# Naming
# New York

# Naming New York

## Manhattan Places &
## How They Got Their Names

Sanna Feirstein

NEW YORK UNIVERSITY PRESS

*New York and London*

NEW YORK UNIVERSITY PRESS
*New York and London*

© 2001 by New York University
All rights reserved

Design by Eliza F. Mayo
Typeset in Rotis and Perpetua

Library of Congress Cataloging-in-Publication Data
Feirstein, Sanna.
Naming New York : Manhattan places and how they got their names /
by Sanna Feirstein
p. cm.
Includes bibliographical references and index.
ISBN 0-8147-2711-5 (cloth : alk. paper) -- ISBN 0-8147-2712-3
(pbk. : alk. paper)
1. Street names--New York (State)--New York--Directories.
2. Streets--New York (State)--New York--Directories.
3. Names, Geographical--New York (State)--New York--Directories.
4. Historic sites--New York (State)--New York--Directories.
5. New York (N.Y.)--History. 6. New York (N.Y.)--Directories. I. Title.
F128.67.A1 F45 2000
917.47'1'0014--dc21                    00-048677

Manufactured in the United States of America

10  9  8  7  6  5  4  3  2  1

*For Sanna Borge*

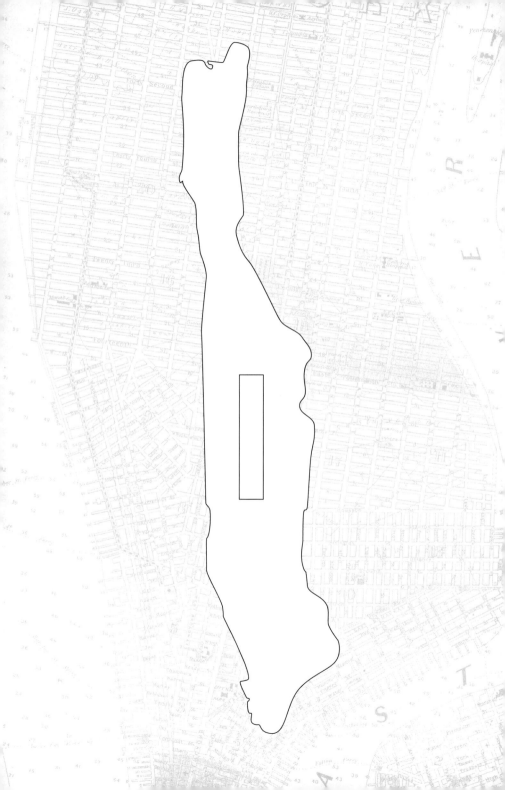

# contents

# acknowledgements

The greatest challenge, as well as the greatest pleasure, involved in compiling this work was the ferreting out of information from a host of sources. Key to this process were the ever-patient staffs of the New-York Historical Society Library, including Alice Gingold whose suggestions gave me a running start; the librarians at the Municipal Reference Library; and Jessica Silver, archivist of Trinity Church. To list the individuals representing a myriad of public and private agencies and organizations who responded to my inquiries in person, via email, or by phone would defy the constraints of space but not desire. Let me express my gratitude to all of those with whom I might not otherwise have come into contact, and who gave their time and shared their knowledge so generously. I was particularly delighted by the many people in the theater industry who enthusiastically contributed facts and color to the why and wherefore of the honorary street names in their district. The phone or email correspondents I would especially like to thank are James Renner, Community Board No.12 District Historian, Rabbi Shlomo Kahn, and the resourceful staff of State Senator Tom Duane. Many hands assisted in the gathering of the images for the book. Among others, I would like to recognize the staff of the New-York Historical Society Print Room and, in particular, Nicole Wells, the Society's Coordinator of Rights and Reproductions; the staff of the Prints and Photographs Department of the Museum of the City of New York; and James Huffman of the Photographs and Prints Division of the New York Public Library Schomburg Center for Research in Black Culture.

This book would never have seen the light of day, nor been the satisfying adventure it has been, without the steadfastly capable, artistic, and organizational talents of Eliza Mayo, designer extraordinaire. I am greatly indebted to Rita Rosenkranz, my agent, for her stalwart, encouraging, and thoughtful mentoring. My editor, Stephen Magro, did an admirable job of guiding this work and its author through the shoals of making a book happen.

The personal and professional support of John Tauranac, Nancy and Natan Wekselbaum, Leni Liftin, and Linda Ferrer were tremendously appreciated. Many thanks to Lucy Mayo and Ethan Feirstein for their interest, assistance, and forbearance as children of an obsessed street walker and talker.

There are no words to express my deep gratitude to Michael Feirstein, chief research assistant, critical reader, tireless booster, and best friend.

# Introduction

Streets and public areas of Manhattan have acquired names for various reasons since shortly after the Dutch established a settlement on the southern tip of the island in the early 17th century. Historically, some names were attached to places to designate a feature of the adjacent landscape: Cherry Street led to a cherry orchard; the Bowery ran through an area set aside in early Dutch days for farm lands, "bowerji" being the Dutch word for farm. Some names derive from early owners of the land on which they are situated: Delancey Street runs through property owned in the 18th century by James de Lancey, son of a Huguenot who emigrated here in the late 17th century; Corlear's Hook is part of the property that belonged to the van Corlear family, 17th-century Dutch settlers.

Early place names were informally bestowed and gained currency through use. With the growth of mechanisms of municipal order, the informal adoption of place names gave way to the official or ceremonial. Government figures, church leaders, and war heroes were honored by having their names conferred on a public place. In more recent times, philanthropists, diplomats, artists, educators, and the like have expanded the list of those recognized on a street, plaza, corner, or even a traffic island.

All of the place names in this book are currently in use. In most, if not all, cases they provide a telling insight into the city's history, both distant and recent. Being aware of the origin of place names can transform a simple neighborhood walk into a trip back through time. One's experience of the city is thus cast in a richer context, expanded to admit awareness of other eras and lives. The city can be thought of as an archeological site—all the layers are here, you just have to know how to read them. Even the plethora of "add-on" place names can acquire meaning with knowledge. Who, for instance, was Gustave Hartman, after whom the square in the East Village was named in 1936? Or Cardinal Stepinac, whose "place" on West 41st Street was named in 1979?

**CAPSULE HISTORY OF MANHATTAN**     By 1574 when Giovanni da Verrazano anchored his ship, the *Dauphine*, in the Lower Bay between today's Staten Island and Brooklyn, Manhattan Island had been home and hunting/planting ground to Native Americans for hundreds of years. Though Verrazano's longboat did not make it to shore due to the threat of a squall, the native Lenapes who had paddled out to investigate his arrival welcomed him as they did Henry Hudson 85 years later. Little did they suspect that the arrival of these strangers on their ancestral lands presaged their doom.

In 1609 Henry Hudson, an English navigator, was employed by the Dutch East India Company to find a northwest passage to the riches of the Far East. Hudson reported back to his employers that, though he had failed in his original mission, he had found a land with riches of a different sort. The shores he had visited offered an abundance of animals—chiefly beaver and otter—whose pelts were of great value to Europeans. Starting in 1622, the Dutch West India Company—a successor to the Dutch East India Company—sent shipments of supplies and settlers to establish outposts of trade in what the Dutch claimed as the province of New Netherland. These outposts were set up on the North (later Hudson) River near Albany, and on the Delaware and Connecticut Rivers. In 1625 Fort Amsterdam was constructed at the southern tip of Manhattan.

The settlement which grew up around this fort was called New Amsterdam and had as its sole mission the development of trade for the profit of the Dutch West India Company. It was a town supporting an impressive array of ethnicities and occupations in which 18 languages were spoken. Dutch control of New Netherland lasted 40 years until 1664 when the British, desirous of uniting their holdings north and south of the Dutch province, took it—effortlessly—for James, Duke of York, brother of King Charles II. One hundred and nineteen years later, the 13 British colonies on North American soil emerged from the yoke of British domination and became part of a new nation.

In the decades following the Revolution, the City of New York—which at the time was defined as the island of Manhattan—became the country's dominant metropolis. It had been the capital of the nation from 1785 to 1790. By 1850 it was the hub of the nation's business activity, supplanting Boston after 1750, Philadelphia by 1790, and Charleston by 1860.

**FROM PATHWAYS TO PLAZAS** Despite the vagaries of war and progress, by the end of the Revolution three principal cultures had laid down physical tracks on the city which would not be eradicated.

The Indians were driven off Manhattan Island, but the trails they cut to traverse it were the foundation of some of the principal north-south thoroughfares used to this day. The Indian names have vanished but the courses of lower and upper Broadway, the Bowery, and St. Nicholas Avenue trace their routes.

The inhabitants living here during the years of Dutch control made use of these trails and contributed their own intricate maze of lanes zigzagging around Fort Amsterdam, many of which survive in today's Financial District. After the British takeover, New York, as it was then called, expanded steadily until the Revolution, by which time the city proper had reached as far north as today's City Hall.

The expansion which preceded the Revolution was hardly preparation for the explosion that followed. By 1807 the city fathers were so confident of, and concerned about, the extent and manner of the future growth of the city that the legislature appointed commissioners to lay out Manhattan above Houston Street in streets, avenues, and squares "to secure a free and abundant circulation of air among said streets and public squares when the same shall be built upon." The area to be so plotted stretched north to 155th Street, it being deemed unlikely that development would ever reach that remote latitude. Needless to say, it was not only to ensure the freedom of the breezes that the commissioners settled on a gridiron plan. Real estate presented in neat rectangular packages was convenient to regulate and to sell. The Commissioners'

Plan unveiled in 1811 was lauded by one observer as having "laid out the highways on the island upon so magnificent a scale, and with so bold a hand, and with such prophetic views, in respect to the future growth and extension of the city, that it will form an ever-lasting monument of the stability and wisdom of the measure."

The new avenues were numbered east to west, the streets south to north. Little open space was left for parks, it being felt that the great bodies of water flowing around the island provided ample natural feast and outlet for the eyes. In the gradual but ruthlessly efficient process of carrying out the plan, and with an ever-vigilant eye to the sale of building lots, the hilly topography of Manhattan south of Morningside Heights was all but leveled.

The Commissioners' Plan was not the first time a city had been plotted by means of a grid, nor the first such layout on Manhattan. Trinity Church, one of the largest city landholders, had begun plotting its property in rectangular blocks by the middle of the 18th century. The Rutgers and Bayard families had laid out their tracts similarly.

Several sections of the city escaped the Commissioners' Plan. The area south of Houston Street was left untouched. The Trinity Church, Rutgers, and Bayard grids survive and retain their original orientations which are at odd angles to the later commissioners' grid. The West Village, having developed its own irregular pathways when it was truly a village physically distinct from the city at the tip of Manhattan, inspired its residents early on to successfully resist the imposition of the grid. Additionally, the diagonal routes of Broadway and the Bowery were such integral parts of the city that the grid was accommodated around them. Stuyvesant Street, the last vestige of Peter Stuyvesant's bowery, and the only street in Manhattan to lie truly east-west, survived because it led to a church.

As mentioned above, the process of labeling the grid's rigidly projected thoroughfares extended only so far as tagging them with numbers. The result of this system was efficient but colorless, though ultimately fortuitous since it left room for subsequent creative alteration.

**NAMING** Prior to the 17th-century governorship of Peter Stuyvesant, the pathways established by the Dutch went nameless. Ever one to bring order out of chaos, Stuyvesant decreed that some streets be named. Many Dutch place names were later adopted and anglicized by the British. Among these are Cliff Street (from Dutch landowner Dirck Van der Clyff), Marketfield Street (from the Dutch Markveldt), the Bowery, Bridge (from the Dutch Brugh)

Street, and Pearl (from the Dutch Perel) Street. It is thought that the name Turtle Bay derives from the Dutch "deutal," meaning knife blade, to describe the shape of its shoreline. Naming streets became a necessity as their numbers and the size of the town increased. The British named places for all manner of things: leaders of Trinity Church, landowners, wives of landowners, physical or topographical characteristics, landmarks, royal personages.

Early names were so informally adopted that two streets with the same name could and did exist at the same time. Official place naming and name changing were documented, somewhat sporadically, in the Minutes of the Common Council starting in 1784, and were mandated for reasons of both local and national import. The outcome of the Revolution inspired a spate of patriotic street name changes in which those smacking of British royalty or nobility were replaced—unimaginatively—with the names of trees. The most notable example of legislated street labels was of course the number system that was part of the Commissioners' Plan. Following the War of 1812, the Common Council formally renamed several streets on today's Lower East Side for heroes of that conflict. Some street names were changed as the result of residents applying to the Common Council for new names, again for various and sundry reasons. One such example was Factory Street, where the residents, caught up in the fashion for the *Waverley* novels of Sir Walter Scott, prevailed on the Council to rename their address Waverly Street (the second "e" was dropped).

Few opportunities remain to name new places in Manhattan, a fact which makes it all the more surprising that occasionally one sees a new street with nothing more for identification than a sign reading "A New Street." In recent decades, new place names have often resulted from the reconfiguration of a space or neighborhood in conjunction with the razing of old structures to make way for the new. The area around the United Nations is one such example, as is the residential development in the West 60s overlooking the Hudson. Much more prevalent than replacing old names with new is the trend to add honorary titles to those names or numbers already in place. Street corners bristle with "add-on" names, some installed so long ago, or at moments whose significance was compelling but so short-lived, that the honoree's identity is lost in the rush of more current events. In some cases this works out for the best as when the honoree of the moment turns out later to have been less than honorable.

The official protocol for designating, adding, or changing a place name is a multistep process. The subject has to be dead and to have had a connection to the block where his or her (or its in the case of an institution) name is to appear. The Department of Transportation also requires that the new name of a place or street honor a cultural or non-profit entity, or a person or event of historical significance. The group sponsoring a sign proposes it to their Community Board. The board votes on it and, if approved, the name is presented to the Parks Committee of the City Council. If approved there, the proposal goes to the full City Council, which votes and passes it along to the mayor. With the mayor's signature, the Department of Transportation is instructed to fabricate and install the sign. In theory, honorary signs are to be in place for a period of 30 days. Practice is a different story. Signs go up far more often than they come down, leaving the city looking like an urban version of Alice's Wonderland. An attempt has been made to give significance to the color of signs. Since 1985, both permanent and "temporary" street signs in Manhattan have been D.O.T. issue green, though some ceremonial street names are displayed on blue signs. The Transportation Department has allowed local business associations such as the Grand Central Partnership and other Business Improvement Districts to select the color of the street signs in their areas so long as they also assume responsibility for the cost, installation, and maintenance of the signs. This accounts for blue signs that are not honorary and for black ones such as those in Lower Manhattan and on Park Avenue in the 60s. Prior to 1985, the street signs of each borough were distinguished by color. Though rarely spotted, yellow signs with black lettering are leftovers from the era when this combination was reserved for Manhattan street signs.

Incredible as it may seem, some New Yorkers ignore the prescribed method of doing things and install signs when, where, and for whom they please.

**THE BOOK** This book is arranged by section of Manhattan, from south to north. The boundaries of the sections were determined by physically exploring them and making a judgement about their parameters based on the cohesiveness of such factors as architecture, use, topography, and subjective "feel." Within each section, the subsections are arranged from east to west. Entries are listed alphabetically by the first letter of the street name. Those looking for Houston Street will find it under East and West Houston Streets as that is how the name appears on the street signs. Streets or places that appear in more than one section of the city will appear in more than one section of the book. The seemingly gay abandon with which the city installs and removes street signs (mostly installs, but construction areas are black holes into which street signs disappear regularly) may cause the occasional blip in the book's roster. It should be noted that playgrounds and structures are not included in this volume.

As with any compilation of this scope, there are bound to be inaccuracies and differences of opinion. It is hoped that these will not detract from the pleasures of exploring the city in a new way.

# Lower Manhattan

TriBeCa

Canal Street

West Street

Church Street

Duane Street

West Broadway

Broadway

Baxter Street

Franklin Street

Civic Center

Park Row

and

Pearl Street

South Street

Robert F. Wagner Sr. Place

Seaport

Park Place

Broadway

Fulton Street

Pearl Street

Battery Park City

West Street

Financial
District

South Street

Fletcher St.

Admiral George Dewey Promenade

# Financial District Manhattan

Island's deep and protected harbor was recognized from the time of the earliest European explorers as a natural phenomenon uniquely suited to the needs of sailing vessels. Unlike the 17th-century settlements in New England which were predicated on religious freedom and established for the purpose of colonization, the Dutch presence in New Amsterdam staked a worldly claim. Since representatives of the Netherlands planted a trading post at the southern tip of Manhattan in 1624, the area's mission as a hub of commerce has remained largely unchanged. Under the British, who peacefully assumed power in New Amsterdam in 1664, trade centered on the East River continued to expand and grew exponentially in the decades following the Revolution. The Financial District's winding streets date from the era when this was the Netherlands' outpost of trade in the New World and testify to their origins as village pathways. Dutch burghers who once bustled about the neigh-

borhood left their names on some streets. Others bear English

translations of Dutch words describing features of the local

topography. Some resonate with references to the prosperous

18th- and 19th-century precursors of today's captains of finance,

while still others hark back to a higher calling, and memorialize

the founders of Trinity Church. Though dwarfed and obscured

in the canyons of the world's financial hub, these tenacious sur-

vivors of days gone by bravely hold their own.

**ADM. GEORGE DEWEY PROMENADE** Dewey, 1837–1917, was a veteran of the Civil
War who, as a naval officer in 1898, achieved renown as "the hero of Manila" in the Spanish-
American War. It was Dewey who gave the famous command, "You may fire when you are
ready, Gridley," and thus destroyed the Spanish fleet in Manila with no loss of American life.
This victory gave the United States its position of power in the Pacific.

**ALBANY STREET** So named as boats running between New York and Albany docked at
this location on the Hudson River in the 19th century.

**ARI HALBERSTAM MEMORIAL RAMP** Named in 1995 for a young Hasidic scholar
who was fatally shot the year before by Lebanese Rashid Baz on this approach from the FDR
Drive to the Brooklyn Bridge. Halberstam was returning from a prayer vigil for the ailing
Lubavitcher Rebbe. The crime was believed to be a reprisal for an attack by an Israeli citizen
on a mosque in Hebron.

**BARCLAY STREET** For Reverend Henry Barclay, 1712–1764, second rector of Trinity
Church. Presiding from 1746 to 1764, Barclay had been a missionary to the Mohawk Indians
and spoke their language as well as Dutch and English.

*The Battery
in the 19th century.*

**BATTERY PLACE & PARK**   For the gun batteries that were constructed here by the British around 1683 to guard the entrance to the Hudson and East Rivers.

**BATTERY PLACE/MERCHANT MARINE VETERANS' PLACE**   Named in 1988 to honor the Merchant Marine Seamen who served in World War II.

**BEAVER STREET**   Named in recognition of the animal whose pelts formed the basis of early trade between the Indians and the Dutch in New Netherland. The fur of beaver and other small animals continued to provide a livelihood to traders into the 19th century, notably John Jacob Astor.

**BOWLING GREEN**   The oldest park in New York City, this open space was used as a parade ground and cattle market in the 17th century. In 1733, three local worthies rented it from the city government for the price of one peppercorn a year and created a bowling green, complete with shaded walks in its precincts.

**BRIDGE STREET**   One of the oldest streets in the city, it was named for the fact that it once led to a bridge which spanned a canal running where Broad Street is now. The name is a translation of the Dutch "Brugh" street.

**BROAD STREET**   Named because it was, indeed, broad. The street ran on either side of a canal which allowed shelter for ships and facilities for off-loading cargo adjacent to warehouses. In the mid-17th century, the canal was filled in, and the two side roads were joined to become one broad thoroughfare.

*Bridge spanning the canal that became Broad Street.*

**BROADWAY** Originally an Indian trail that ran north from the southern tip of Manhattan, Broadway now extends from the Battery into the Bronx. The street's name derives from its unusual width.

**CARLISLE STREET** No reliable attribution for this name has been found.

**CEDAR STREET** Previously Little Queen Street, this was one of many streets whose names were changed after the Revolution in an effort to expunge any association with the British royals.

**CHURCH STREET** The street takes its name from the fact that it runs through land granted to Trinity Church by Queen Anne in 1705. The tract, extending west of Broadway to the river, and from approximately Fulton to Christopher Streets, had previously been known as the Queen's (later King's) farm.

**CLIFF STREET** For Dirck Van der Clyff, a Dutch settler through whose property the street was opened.

**COENTIES ALLEY & SLIP** The name derives from the nickname given Dutch tanner and shoemaker Coenraet Ten Eyck who owned property in the vicinity.

**CORTLANDT STREET** For Oloff Van Cortlandt, an early Dutch settler and leading citizen of New Amsterdam who owned the land here.

**DEY STREET** For Dutch settler Theunis Dey, gardener and miller, through whose farm the street was laid.

**DUTCH STREET** Though the street existed earlier, its name first appeared on a map of 1789. The name may derive from the street's proximity to the Old North Dutch Church which stood on the west side of William Street between Ann and Fulton Streets from 1769 to 1875.

**EDGAR STREET** Though there is little documentation, one source asserts this street was named for William Edgar, an 18th-century merchant.

**EXCHANGE ALLEY** The extension of Exchange Place from Broadway to Trinity Place.

**EXCHANGE PLACE** For the Merchants' Exchange Building which was located on adjacent Wall Street in the mid-19th century.

*Old North Dutch Church*

**FLETCHER STREET**   For Colonel Benjamin Fletcher, British colonial governor, 1692–1698. Trinity Church records credit Fletcher with awarding to the church the patent for drift whales. This boon allowed Trinity to raise money for the construction of its first church through the sale of any whales which drifted to shore. Fletcher was involved in granting Trinity its charter in 1697, the same year he was ordered back to England for his activities in encouraging New York merchants to engage in privateering during King William's War.

**FRONT STREET**   In the 18th century, landfill extended Manhattan Island farther into the East River, first beyond Pearl Street, the original riverside road, to Water Street. Subsequent landfill brought the shore to this point, making Front the street that ran along the water's edge.

*Fulton's steamship* Clermont.

**FULTON STREET**   Named for Robert Fulton, 1765–1815, designer of the steamship *Clermont* which ran between New York and Albany starting in 1807.

**GOLD STREET**   A shortening of the original name of the area, Golden Hill, referring to the color of the wheat grown locally. Appropriately, a gold market was located here after the Revolution until 1930, as, at one time, was the Federal Reserve Bank.

**GOUVERNEUR LANE**   For Nicholas Gouverneur, respected 18th century merchant who released the land for the street in 1798.

**GREENWICH STREET**   One of the earliest roads to run from the Battery to 14th Street, it was named for the village to which it led. The street was created on landfill carried out intermittently from 1739 to 1785.

**HANOVER STREET & SQUARE**   Surviving the post-Revolutionary purge of British royal names, these recall the Hanoverian origins of England's King George I.

**JOHN STREET**   The eponymous John was one John Harpendingh, a 17th-century shoe maker who, along with others of his trade, owned the land here which came to be called "Shoemaker's Pasture." Tanneries were gradually forced to move north and west of the city, due to the unpleasant odors they produced. Harpendingh's will donated the land for the North Dutch Church.

**JOSEPH P. WARD STREET**   Named in 1967 to honor a much-decorated World War II radio navigator.

Financial District

**LEGION MEMORIAL SQUARE**  Named in 1933 in recognition of the American Legion, the largest veterans' organization in the United States. The Legion seeks to further the interests and rights of veterans of wars in which American soldiers saw action.

**LIBERTY STREET & PLACE**  In 1794 Crown Street was changed to Liberty Street in the post-Revolution effort to erase references to British royalty. Presumably this applied to the adjacent Liberty Place as well.

**LOUISE NEVELSON PLAZA**  Named in 1978 to honor the acclaimed Russian-born sculptress. Four of her works adorn the space.

**MAIDEN LANE**  Translated from the Dutch word for maiden, this street acquired its name from the fact that a stream ran through it in which Dutch women washed their clothes.

**MARKETFIELD STREET**  Another name translated from the original Dutch, this street is said to have run to the marketplace located in what was later Bowling Green.

**MILL LANE**  The street followed a small stream on which a water mill was built. The mill was associated with the early Jewish community which in 1730 erected Congregation Shearith Israel, the first synagogue in the city, near this location.

**MOORE STREET**  A misspelling of this street's name has allegedly given rise to an erroneous attribution of its derivation. This was the location where boats were moored before landfill extended the island into the rivers. The final "e" was added to the name over time on the mistaken assumption that the street was named for a member of a Moore family.

**MORRIS STREET**  It is believed that this street was named for a member of the family of Gouverneur Morris, 1752–1816, politician and diplomat.

**NASSAU STREET**  Named before 1696 for the Dutch Prince William of Nassau who became King William III of England, Scotland, and Ireland in 1689.

**NEW STREET**  So named as it was the first street opened after the British seized the city in 1664.

**OLD SLIP**  Thus identified on maps since the early 18th century, the name reflects the fact that the street was one of the city's early boat slips.

*Old Slip, ca. 1905*

**PARK PLACE**  Probably named because at the end of the 18th century the area around what is now City Hall became a fashionable residential district, with the Common (now City Hall Park) being known as The Park.

**PEARL STREET**  Named for the oyster shells left in the area by the native Lenape Indians. Before landfill extended Manhattan island into the East River in the18th century, this was the waterfront road.

*Oyster shells gave Pearl Street its name*

**PETER MINUIT PLAZA**  Minuit, 1580–1638, was the Dutch governor of New Netherland credited with the "purchase" of Manhattan Island from the Indians.

**PIERRE TOUSSAINT SQUARE**  Named in 1989 for the slave who arrived in New York from Haiti in 1787 and became a successful hairdresser, supporting his widowed employer and her family with his earnings. Freed in 1807, Toussaint was noted for his generosity to Catholic charities.

**PINE STREET**  As with other tree-named streets, this one was changed from King Street in 1794 to remove the reference to the British royals.

**PLATT STREET**  For John (or Jacob depending on the source) S. Platt, merchant, through whose property the street was laid in 1834.

*Pierre Toussaint*

**RECTOR STREET**  For the rectors of the first Trinity Church, erected in 1698, who lived on the street.

**ROBERT F. WAGNER JR. PARK**  Robert Wagner, Jr. (III until his father's death), 1944–1993, was the son of three-time Mayor Robert F. Wagner, 1910–1991, and grandson of Robert F. Wagner, Sr., 1877–1953, state and U.S. senator and justice of the New York State Supreme Court. The younger Wagner served the city in several capacities, among them as a member of the City Council, chairman of the City Planning Commission, and president of the Board of Education.

**RYDERS ALLEY**  No reliable attribution for this name has been found.

**SOUTH STREET**  In the 18th century, landfill extended the shoreline of Manhattan island into the East River, first past Pearl Street, and later beyond the line of Water Street. Subsequent expansion pushed the shoreline past Front Street, creating a waterfront with South Street running along the river's edge.

**SOUTH WILLIAM STREET**  The southern portion of William Street (see below).

Financial District

29

**STATE STREET** Originally Copsey Street, the name was changed in 1793 in reference to the State House (also called Government House) erected here in 1790 on the site of Fort Amsterdam. The next and present building on the site is Cass Gilbert's U.S. Custom House, completed in 1907, now home to the Museum of the American Indian.

**STONE STREET** Sources vary as to whether this was the first or the second Dutch street to be paved with blocks of stone, thus earning the name.

*Trinity Church*

**TEDDY GLEASON STREET** Named in 1997 for the longshoreman and labor leader who was affiliated with the International Longshoremen's Association and served as its president for 25 years. Gleason died in 1992.

**TEMPLE STREET** All that remains of this street is a sign pointing south across the middle of Liberty Place. The name derives either from the fact that it once led to Trinity Church, or from Sir John Temple, the first British consul general appointed to the United States after the Revolution, and resident of nearby Greenwich Street.

**THAMES STREET** Named to recall the English river, the land for the street was ceded to the city by a member of the Bayard family in 1749.

**TRINITY PLACE** Named for adjacent Trinity Church.

**VESEY STREET** For the Reverend William Vesey, who served from 1697 to 1746 as the first rector of Trinity Church. Vesey founded a school for slaves and Indians and helped establish the Charity School, currently known as Trinity School, now located on West 91st Street.

**VIETNAM VETERANS PLAZA** Named in 1982 as a memorial to the 250,000 New York City residents who served during this war, over 1,700 of whom died in the conflict.

**WALL STREET** Wall Street follows the line of the palisade wall that the Dutch erected across the northern perimeter of New Amsterdam in 1653 to protect against attack from the British New Englanders.

**WASHINGTON STREET** For President George Washington, 1732–1799.

**WATER STREET** As per the above South Street entry, Water Street was the first new shoreline road created on 18th-century landfill.

**WEST STREET** Built on 18th-century landfill, this street was named in anticipation that no thoroughfare would exist farther west.

**WHITEHALL STREET** For the white mansion built here for Peter Stuyvesant, 1610–1672, the last Dutch governor of New Netherland.

**WILLIAM STREET** For William Beeckman, 1623–1707, wealthy landowner and progenitor of the Beekman family in America.

**WUI PLAZA** Though longer names are spelled out on other signs throughout the city, initials are used here for Western Union International. The company was headquartered on this block into the 1980s.

*The palisade wall that gave Wall Street its name.*

# Battery Park City Built on landfill,

some of which came from the excavation for the World
Trade Center, this 92-acre complex was designed for both
residential and commercial use. An example of creative re-use
of the Hudson River waterfront, the "city" was made possible
by the transition to containerized shipping activity on the river,
and the resulting obsolescence of existing shipping facilities.
Centered around the World Financial Center, and constructed
for the most part in the 1980s and 1990s, the area features
parks, a marina, and museums. With the exception of North
and South End Avenues whose names are self-explanatory, the
street plan and names continue those of the adjacent Financial
District. A separate listing of the streets will not therefore be
given here.

# Civic Center & South Street Seaport

Just to the north of the city's money market is its court system and local seat of municipal, state, and federal government. The Civic Center hums with lawyers, litigants, defendants, bureaucrats, and the legions of civil and legal staffs that support them. Until the early 18th century, the neighborhood was dominated by "Collect" or "Fresh Water" Pond, a favorite recreation spot. With the 1811 completion of City Hall on the Common, considered at the time to be the northern fringe of the city, the area's lot as the city's administrative nerve center was cast. Monumental edifices of varying vintages and styles now crowd the French-inspired City Hall and its once bucolic park, and the Brooklyn Bridge looms not far to the east. Until rescued and rehabilitated in the early 1980s by a combination of public and private efforts, the adjacent South Street Seaport was a crumbling vestige of the lower East River's glory days. In the

first half of the 19th century these riverside streets bustled

with ships' captains, sailors, and all the trades that supported

commerce by tall ship. By the end of the 19th century, shipping

was migrating to the deeper Hudson River waterfront, leaving

the South Street area to decay. Some 30 years later a citizens'

group mobilized to preserve the historic buildings and, with

the opening of the South Street Seaport Museum in 1967, the

reinvention of this fascinating locale was set in motion.

**ANN STREET**  Two sources give varying attributions: one traces the name to the wife of prominent colonial merchant Thomas White; the other to a member of the Beekman family. As the Beekmans owned land in the vicinity, and as Ann Street is one block south of Beekman Street, the second derivation seems more likely.

**AVENUE OF THE FINEST**  Named in 1969 in recognition of the New York City Police whose headquarters is nearby.

**AVENUE OF THE STRONGEST**  Named in 1996 in honor of the men and women of the city's Department of Sanitation after a winter of 16 snowstorms during which they plowed 7½ feet of snow from city streets. The headquarters of the Department of Sanitation is on Worth Street.

*Police officer from the 19th century.*

**BACHE PLAZA**  The building opposite this small intersection housed the investment company Bache & Company until it was acquired by Prudential Securities in the early 1980s.

**BAXTER STREET** Named in 1853 for Lieutenant Colonel Charles Baxter, a hero of the Mexican War killed at Chapultepec in 1847.

**BEEKMAN STREET** For William Beeckman, 1623–1707, wealthy landowner and progenitor of the Beekman family in America.

**BENSON PLACE** For Egbert Benson who was appointed first attorney general of New York State in 1777, and served as first president of the New-York Historical Society.

**BROADWAY** Originally an Indian trail that ran north from the southern tip of Manhattan, Broadway now extends from the Battery into the Bronx. The street's name derives from its unusual width.

**BURLING SLIP** Originally the name of the East River end of John Street, the Burlings being early merchants in the seaport area. In a 1986 application to the City Council, the South Street Seaport Museum proposed reinstating the name at the eastern end of John Street to "reflect the original purpose and character of the street, and to reinforce people's awareness of the Seaport district's history as the city's first port."

**CANAL STREET** The street was originally a stream that ran from what was once "Fresh Water," or "Collect," Pond, north of present-day City Hall, to the Hudson River. By the early 19th century, in the wake of a yellow fever epidemic, the pond had become seriously polluted and was identified as a health hazard. In 1805, to drain off the pond, the stream was widened into a canal—hence the name—and both were filled in over a decade later.

**CARDINAL HAYES PLACE** For Cardinal Patrick Joseph Hayes, 1867–1938. Hayes was an altar boy and received his first sacrament at the original St. Andrew's Church which was located where the Federal Courthouse is now. The sanctuary of the church rests on the site of the building where the cardinal was born.

**CATHERINE LANE** Possibly of the same origin as the Catherine Street and Slip in Chinatown which were named for Catherine DesBrosses, daughter of Jacques (James) DesBrosses, 17th-century Huguenot immigrant whose rum distillery was located near the East River.

**CENTRE STREET** Originally called Collect Street, this street was laid over Collect Pond which was filled in early in the 19th century. The street name was changed in 1828 to identify it as terminating at the Centre Market. Note the British spelling of the name.

**CHAMBERS STREET** For John Chambers, pre-Revolutionary barrister, alderman, corporation counsel, and member of the governor's council. In 1751, Chambers was appointed justice of the colonial supreme court of judicature. He died in 1764.

**CHURCH STREET** The street takes its name from the fact that it runs through land granted to Trinity Church by Queen Anne in 1705. The tract, extending west of Broadway to the river, and from approximately Fulton to Christopher Streets, had previously been known as the Queen's (later King's) farm.

**CITY HALL PARK** Originally called the Common, and at various times in the 18th century considered the northern boundary of the city, this open space was the site of the city's first almshouse, a military barracks, gallows, and burying ground. With the completion of the present City Hall here in 1811, the name of the public area around it was changed to reflect its new status.

*City Hall, completed 1811.*

**CLIFF STREET** For Dirck Van der Clyff, a Dutch settler through whose property the street was opened.

**COLLECT POND PARK** This was originally the site of a large freshwater pond which was a favorite 18th-century recreation destination. The name was an inaccurate rendition of the Dutch word kalch, meaning lime—a reference to the oyster shells left here by Indians. By the end of the 18th century the pond had become polluted and was filled in by 1811.

**CORTLANDT ALLEY** For Oloff Van Cortlandt, an early Dutch settler and leading citizen of New Amsterdam who owned the land in this general vicinity.

**DOVER STREET** No definitive origin exists for this street name, but one source notes that in the 18th century, English men-of-war ships docked at the foot of the street. It is possible that British sailors named the street to recall the coastal town in their homeland.

**DRUMGOOLE SQUARE** Named in 1989 for John Christopher Drumgoole, 1816–1888, an Irish immigrant who studied for the priesthood in midlife and devoted his efforts to helping homeless boys. He built the Mission of the Immaculate Virgin which provided a home for 2,000 homeless working boys, mostly bootblacks and newsboys. Drumgoole was known as the hero of New York's newsboys.

**DUANE STREET** For James Duane, 1733–1797, a lawyer who was appointed mayor of the city in 1783, thereby becoming the first to serve in that office after the evacuation of the British forces from New York.

**ELK STREET** Named to honor the Benevolent and Protective Order of Elks which was founded on this street in 1867 by Charles S. Vivian and some fellow actors. It is suspected that their primary motive was to bypass the Sunday dry laws. Since that time the Elks has evolved into a national charitable organization which supports disabled children, provides entertainment to veterans' hospitals, and grants scholarships.

*The seal of the Benevolent and Protective Order of Elks.*

**FEDERAL PLAZA** The open plaza area fronting the Jacob K. Javits Federal Building and the United States Court of International Trade Building.

**FISHBRIDGE PARK** Located between the Fulton Fish Market and the Brooklyn Bridge, this former parking lot and garbage dump was salvaged by volunteers in the early 1990s. Taking its name from the adjacent landmarks, it was officially designated as New York City parkland in 1997.

**FLETCHER STREET** For Colonel Benjamin Fletcher, British colonial governor, 1692–1698. Trinity Church records credit Fletcher with awarding to the church the patent for drift whales. This boon allowed Trinity to raise money for the construction of its first church through the sale of any whales which drifted to shore. Fletcher was involved in granting Trinity its charter in 1697, the same year he was ordered back to England for his activities in encouraging New York merchants to engage in privateering during King William's War.

**FOLEY SQUARE** Named in 1926 for Thomas "Big Tom" Foley, 1852–1925, leader of the city's Democratic machine.

**FRANKFORT STREET** Named to honor the native city of Jacob Leisler, self-appointed lieutenant governor of New York from 1689 to 1691. As a result of the Glorious Revolution in England which overthrew Catholic James II in 1688, anti-Catholic Jacob Leisler took command of the province anticipating that Protestant William of Orange would ascend to the British throne and become the colony's sovereign. Leisler was later hanged when the forces of King William turned against him. Leisler owned land in this area and is said to have been buried here after his execution.

**FRANKLIN STREET** Named in 1777 for inventor and statesman Benjamin Franklin, 1706–1790.

**FRONT STREET**  In the 18th century, landfill extended Manhattan Island farther into the East River, first beyond Pearl Street, the original riverside road, to Water Street. Subsequent landfill brought the shore to this point, making Front the street that ran along the water's edge.

**FULTON STREET**  Named for Robert Fulton, 1765–1815, designer of the steamship *Clermont* which ran between New York and Albany starting in 1807.

**GOLD STREET**  A shortening of the original name of the area, Golden Hill, referring to the color of the wheat grown locally. Appropriately, a gold market was located here after the Revolution until 1930, as, at one time, was the Federal Reserve Bank.

**HOGAN PLACE**  Named in 1980 for Manhattan District Attorney Frank Hogan, who died in 1974 after 32 years in office.

**JOHN DeLURY SR. PLAZA**  For the 1930s driver and garbage handler who organized the labor organization that later became the Uniformed Sanitationmen's Association.

**JOHN J. CLAVIN PLACE**  Named in 1989 for an employee of the Department of Corrections who, until his death in 1986, devoted his spare time to advocating for the homeless.

**JOHN STREET**  The eponymous John was one John Harpendingh, a 17th-century shoe-maker who, along with others of his trade, owned the land here which came to be called "Shoemaker's Pasture." Tanneries were gradually forced to move north and west of the city, due to the unpleasant odors they produced. Harpendingh's will donated the land for the North Dutch Church.

**JOSEPH DOHERTY CORNER**  This corner was named in 1990 to recognize an immigrant from the United Kingdom who, at the time, had been in prison in this country since 1983, making him the longest-held prisoner in the history of the Metropolitan Correction Center. Doherty had escaped from a Northern Ireland prison where he was being held on charges connected with the murder of a British soldier in Belfast in 1980. Britain's demand for his extradition was denied by the U.S. on the basis that the acts for which he was wanted in the U.K. were political, not common crimes. The way was cleared for his extradition in January of 1992.

**LAFAYETTE STREET**  Named in 1825 by John Jacob Astor, through whose land the street was laid. Astor wished to honor the Marquis de Lafayette, the Revolutionary War hero, who had recently revisited the city.

**LEONARD STREET**  For one of the three sons of French Huguenot Anthony Lispenard, 1683–1755, merchant and landowner in Lower Manhattan. Through marriage into the Rutgers family, Leonard became one of the largest landowners in the city.

**MADISON STREET** For James Madison, 1751–1836, fourth president of the United States.

**MURRAY STREET** Sources vary as to whether the street is named for Joseph Murray, a prominent lawyer who lived on lower Broadway, or for Robert Murray, vestryman of Trinity Church and one of the first trustees of King's (Columbia) College who owned property in Kips Bay.

**NASSAU STREET** Named by 1696 for the Dutch Prince William of Nassau who became King William III of England, Scotland, and Ireland in 1689.

*James Madison*

**PARK PLACE** Probably named because at the end of the 18th century the area around what is now City Hall became a fashionable residential district, with the Common (now City Hall Park) being known as The Park.

**PARK ROW** Originally Chatham Street, but changed in the first quarter of the 19th century presumably to note its path along one side of City Hall Park. City Hall itself was completed in 1811.

**PEARL STREET** Named for the oyster shells left in the area by the native Lenape Indians Before landfill extended Manhattan Island into the East River in the 18th century, this was the waterfront road.

**PECK SLIP** For Benjamin Peck, 18th-century merchant. This slip was used for the earliest Brooklyn ferry.

**POLICE PLAZA** The open plaza area surrounding the headquarters of the New York City Police Department.

**READE STREET** For John Reade, mid-18th-century vestryman and warden of Trinity Church.

**ROBERT F. WAGNER SR. PLACE** Wagner, 1877–1953, was a German immigrant and politician who was father and grandfather to two other politicians of the same name. Wagner senior served as state senator in 1908, justice of the New York State Supreme Court from 1918 to 1926, and as U.S. senator in 1926.

**ROSE STREET** Originally Prince Street, the name was changed in 1794, probably in response to anti royal fervor after the Revolution. One source associates the name with a Captain Joseph Rose, a merchant who died in 1807.

**SOUTH STREET**  In the 18th century, landfill extended the shoreline of Manhattan Island into the East River, first past Pearl Street, and later beyond the line of Water Street. Subsequent expansion pushed the shoreline past Front Street, creating a waterfront with South Street running along the river's edge.

**SPRUCE STREET**  The street was previously named George Street and was probably changed after the Revolution to erase its association with the British royal house. Many streets currently named for trees had prior names with royal associations.

**STEVE FLANDERS SQUARE**  Named in 1984 for a news reporter who, when he died in 1983, was chief political reporter for WCBS Radio.

**THEATRE ALLEY**  Named for its proximity to the Park Theatre which was built nearby in 1798 and destroyed by fire in 1848. The original British spelling remains.

**THOMAS PAINE PARK**  Named in 1977 for the political theorist and writer. In 1776 Paine published the essay *Common Sense* which stirred the patriot cause at the time of the Revolution.

**THOMAS STREET**  For one of the three sons of French Huguenot Anthony Lispenard, 1683–1755, merchant and landowner in lower Manhattan.

*Thomas Paine's essay* Common Sense.

**TRIMBLE PLACE**  This short street was once a road leading to the New York Hospital which was located in the area bounded by Duane, Broadway, Church, and present-day Worth Streets. George T. Trimble and his son Merritt both served as president of the hospital in the early to mid-19th century.

**WALKER STREET**  For Benjamin Walker, appointed Naval Officer of New York by George Washington.

**WARREN STREET**  For Admiral Sir Peter Warren, commander of the British naval forces stationed in New York in the 1730s. Warren acquired several hundred acres in Greenwich (now Village) in the 1740s.

**WATER STREET**  As per the above South Street entry, Water Street was the first new shore-line road created on 18th-century landfill.

**WEST BROADWAY**  A broad way west of Broadway.

**WHITE STREET**  For Captain Thomas White, who settled in New York in the mid-18th century and traded in imported teas.

**WILLIAM STREET**  For William Beeckman, 1623–1707, wealthy landowner and progenitor of the Beekman family in America.

**WORTH STREET**  For Major General William Jenkins Worth, 1794–1849, second in command to Zachary Taylor in the Mexican War. Worth is said to have been the first to plant the American flag at the Rio Grande. He died in this conflict and is buried in Worth Square (see NoMad). Worth's valor inspired the name of Fort Worth, Texas.

*William Jenkins Worth*

# TriBeCa

The name TriBeCa, adopted in the mid-1970s, is an acronym for the TRIangle BElow CAnal street. In 1705, Queen Anne granted this area, which until that time had been part of what was called the Queen's Farm (later King's Farm), to Trinity Church. Recognizing that the city was moving ever northward from the business center at the island's southern tip, the church cannily developed much of its property in a grid street pattern, one of the first seen in Manhattan, and set about building row houses for use by the middle class. Trinity thus set the pace for its growth into one of the city's greatest landholders. In the 19th century, commerce found its way here and merchants put up capacious loft buildings for manufacturing and warehousing. The busy waterfront piers and properties became the hub of the dairy, coffee, tea, and spice trade that supplied the city's markets. In the continual rotation which defines land use in Manhattan, these commercial centers were left behind in the scramble uptown, only to be seized upon in the 1960s by artists needing large, inexpensive, and unobstructed spaces for their work. Currently a mixed-use neighborhood, TriBeCa retains some manufacturing, but is sought mostly for its rash of new and trendy restaurants, stores, and galleries downstairs from super high-end residential spreads.

AVENUE OF THE AMERICAS   In 1945, Mayor Fiorello La Guardia added this designation to the name of 6th Avenue to honor the ideals shared by this country and our sister pan-American nations.

BEACH STREET   The street was originally spelled Bache, and was named for Paul Bache, the son-in-law of French Huguenot merchant Anthony Lispenard, 1683–1755.

BROADWAY   Originally an Indian trail that ran north from the southern tip of Manhattan, Broadway now extends from the Battery into the Bronx. The street's name derives from its unusual width.

CANAL STREET   The street was originally a stream that ran from what was once "Fresh Water," or "Collect," Pond, north of present-day City Hall, to the Hudson River. By the early 19th century, in the wake of a yellow fever epidemic, the pond had become seriously polluted and was identified as a health hazard. In 1805, to drain off the pond, the stream was widened into a canal—hence the name—and both were filled in over a decade later.

CHAMBERS STREET   For John Chambers, pre-Revolutionary barrister, alderman, corporation counsel, and member of the provincial governor's council. In 1751 Chambers was appointed justice of the colonial supreme court of judicature. Chambers died in 1764.

CHURCH STREET   The street takes its name from the fact that it runs through land granted to Trinity Church by Queen Anne in 1705. The tract, extending west of Broadway to the river, and from approximately Fulton to Christopher Streets, had previously been known as the Queen's (later King's) farm.

**COLLISTER STREET** Thomas Collister is listed in the city directories for 1793, 1794, and 1797 as sexton of Trinity Church. The street's location on original Trinity Church property suggests that it was named to honor this member of the Trinity community.

**DESBROSSES STREET** For merchant Elias DesBrosses, 1718–1778, warden of Trinity Church, and import/export dealer who specialized in trade with Madeira and the West Indies. DesBrosses was a son of 17th-century Huguenot immigrant Jacques (James) DesBrosses whose rum distillery was located on the East River (see Chinatown for Elias's sister Catherine and brothers James and Oliver).

**DUANE STREET & PARK** For James Duane, 1733–1797, a lawyer who was appointed mayor of the city in 1783 thereby becoming the first to serve in that office after the evacuation of the British forces from New York. The city paid Trinity Church the equivalent of $5.00 for the park in 1797.

**ERICSSON PLACE** For John Ericsson, 1803–1889, Swedish immigrant best known for his 1862 design of the *Monitor*, one of the first ironclad warships. The ship saw duty during the Civil War and was only one of Ericsson's many inventions which included the screw propeller, a device which replaced ships' paddle wheels. Ericsson was a resident of this part of the city, and his statue stands in Battery Park.

*John Ericsson*

**FRANKLIN STREET & PLACE** Named in 1777 for inventor and statesman Benjamin Franklin, 1706–1790.

**GREENWICH STREET** One of the earliest roads to run from the Battery to 14th Street, it was named for the village to which it led. The street was created on landfill carried out intermittently from 1739 to 1785.

**HARRISON STREET** For George Harrison, whose brewery stood near this location in the mid-18th century. Some of the Federal-style houses on this street were moved here from an obliterated portion of Washington Street.

**HUBERT STREET** For Hubert Van Wagenen, vestryman of Trinity Church from 1787 to 1806.

**HUDSON RIVER PARK** The area between the Joe DiMaggio Highway and the Hudson River which is being developed as parkland from Chambers Street to 59th Street.

**HUDSON STREET** Named for the fact that it parallels the river nearby.

**JAMES BOGARDUS TRIANGLE**  Named in 1989 for the inventor, engineer, and architect who advocated the use of cast iron for entire buildings. Bogardus, 1800–1874, was a major influence on New York City's boom in cast-iron construction which lasted from mid-century to around 1880. SoHo boasts the largest concentration of full or partial cast-iron buildings in the world.

John Jay

**JAY STREET**  For statesman and jurist John Jay, 1745–1829. In 1789 Jay was appointed by George Washington to be the first chief justice of the United States. He negotiated the Jay Treaty which ended the Revolution and served two terms as governor of New York State.

**LAIGHT STREET**  For William Laight, leading 18th-century merchant and patriot during the War of Independence.

**LEONARD STREET**  For one of the three sons of French Huguenot Anthony Lispenard, 1683–1755, merchant and landowner in Lower Manhattan. Through marriage into the Rutgers family, Leonard became one of the largest landowners in the city.

**LISPENARD STREET**  For the Lispenard family whose property was in this vicinity. Part of their holdings, known as Lispenard Meadows, or Lispenard Swamp, was a wetland held responsible by some for contributing to the devastating periodic outbreaks of mosquito-borne disease.

**MURRAY STREET**  Sources vary as to whether the street is named for Joseph Murray, a prominent lawyer who lived on lower Broadway, or for Robert Murray, vestryman of Trinity Church, and one of the first trustees of King's (Columbia) College who owned property in Kips Bay.

**NORTH MOORE STREET**  For Bishop Benjamin Moore, who served as sixth rector of Trinity Church from 1806 to 1816, and as president of King's (Columbia) College. Moore's son, Clement Clark Moore, wrote *'Twas the Night Before Christmas.* The "North" was added to differentiate this street from the preexisting Moore Street in the Financial District.

**PARK PLACE**  Probably named because at the end of the 18th century the area around what is now City Hall became a fashionable residential district, with the Common (now City Hall Park) being known as The Park.

**READE STREET**  For John Reade, mid-18th century vestryman and warden of Trinity Church.

*St. John's Chapel*

**ST. JOHN'S LANE** This street is a remnant of St. John's Park, a fashionable residential enclave in the 1820s, 1830s, and 1840s. Attracted by St. John's Chapel, built in 1807 as a parish of Trinity Church, well-to-do families put up fine row houses centered on a private park. All this gentility came to an end with the approach of commerce from the south, and was dealt a death blow when Commodore Vanderbilt purchased the park in 1866 in order to build his Hudson Terminal freight yard. This erstwhile bucolic Federal-style neighborhood is now the Holland Tunnel exit rotary.

**SERGEANT FINBAR DEVINE CORNER** Named for a 35-year veteran of the Police Department who died in 1995. According to the City Council proceedings honoring him, Devine was "a fervent supporter and co-founder of the New York City Police Dept. Emerald Society," as well as drum major of its pipe and drum band.

**STAPLE STREET** Two possible derivations for the name of this street: one source attributes it to the fact that New Amsterdam was granted the "staple" right for the colony of New Netherland on the sale of tobacco. According to Dutch tradition, any ship which refused to pay duty on its cargo had that cargo unloaded and put up "in staples" for public sale. Alternatively, the name may be a remnant of the time when the Duane Park area was the city's butter, egg, and cheese market; hence, grocery "staples" were shipped here for sale.

**THOMAS STREET** For one of the three sons of French Huguenot Anthony Lispenard, 1683–1755, merchant and landowner in lower Manhattan.

**TRIBECA PARK** Named for the area in which it is located.

**VARICK STREET** For Colonel Richard Varick, George Washington's secretary, and later city recorder. Varick was appointed mayor of the city by Governor George Clinton in 1789.

**VESTRY STREET** Variously explained as being named for the vestry of Trinity Church, or for the vestry house of St. John's Chapel erected nearby in 1807.

**WALKER STREET** For Benjamin Walker, appointed Naval Officer of New York by George Washington.

**WARREN STREET** For Admiral Sir Peter Warren, commander of the British naval forces stationed in New York in the 1730s. Warren acquired several hundred acres in Greenwich (now Village) in the 1740s.

**WASHINGTON MARKET PARK**  Created in 1983 and named for a market that stood at Washington, Vesey, and Fulton Streets from 1812 until 1859 when it was shut down due to traffic congestion and corruption. The original market location was revived from 1883 until 1956 when its wholesale facilities moved to Hunts Point in the Bronx.

**WASHINGTON STREET**  For President George Washington, 1732–1799.

**WATTS STREET**  For merchant John Watts, a founder of the Leake and Watts Orphan Asylum, opened 1830–1831.

**WEST BROADWAY**  A broad way west of Broadway.

**WEST STREET**  Built on 18th-century landfill, this street was named in the certainty that no thoroughfare would exist farther west.

**WHITE STREET**  For Captain Thomas White who settled in New York in the mid-18th century and traded in imported teas.

**WORTH STREET**  Named for Major General William Jenkins Worth, 1794–1849, second in command to Zachary Taylor in the Mexican War. Said to have been the first to plant the American flag at the Rio Grande, Worth died in this conflict and is buried in Worth Square (see NoMad). Worth's valor is memorialized in the name of Fort Worth, Texas.

**WORTH STREET / JUSTICE JOHN M. HARLAN WAY**  This section of Worth Street was named in 1991 to honor the associate United States Supreme Court Justice, 1833–1911, on the 100th anniversary of the adjacent New York Law School from which Harlan graduated in 1924.

**YORK STREET**  For James, Duke of York, 1633–1701. In 1664, James persuaded his older brother, King Charles II of England, to grant him the province of New Netherland. James sent Colonel Richard Nicolls to take the colony from the Dutch, which he did, with the only casualty being the fury of Dutch Governor Peter Stuyvesant. James gave his title to the colony, the city, and this street.

# Mid-Lower Manhattan

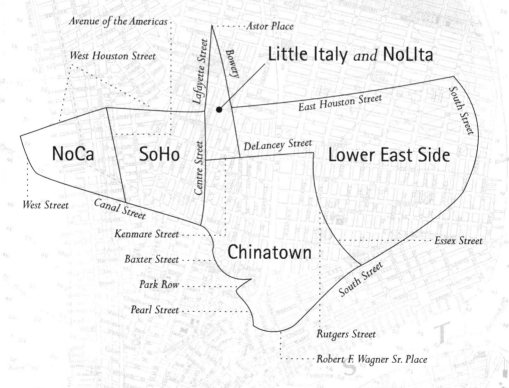

Avenue of the Americas

Astor Place

West Houston Street

*Lafayette Street*

*Bowery*

## Little Italy *and* NoLIta

*East Houston Street*

*South Street*

## NoCa     ## SoHo

*Centre Street*

*DeLancey Street*

## Lower East Side

West Street

*Canal Street*

Kenmare Street

Baxter Street

## Chinatown

Essex Street

Park Row

*South Street*

Pearl Street

Rutgers Street

Robert F. Wagner Sr. Place

# Lower East Side The Lower East Side

is a part of New York that has come to symbolize the influx of immigrants to the city in the 19th century. Prior to the American Revolution, the area consisted of farmland owned by wealthy landholders. After the war, much of the land was broken up into small lots, typically 25 feet wide by 100 feet deep, which were bought and built on by merchants, lawyers, and craftsmen. Over time, the bustle of commerce pushed these prosperous citizens ever farther north to less developed, more genteel surroundings. Waves of immigrants, first from Ireland, then Italy and eastern Europe took their places, over-flowing the tenements that strained to house them in the mid-19th century. The rampant poverty and deplorable health con-ditions that proliferated here were chronicled in the descrip-tions and photographs of journalist, photographer, and reformer Jacob Riis. All this began to change in the late 19th century and into the 20th, as efforts by social service organi-

zations and slum-clearance projects were mobilized to address

this urban blight. The neighborhood maintains its historic rep-

utation for discount shopping and ethnic diversity, now adding

burgeoning gentrification to the mix.

**ABRAHAM KAZAN STREET** For Abraham E. Kazan, 1889–1971, who, as president of the Amalgamated Clothing Workers Housing Corporation, engineered the building of affordable housing for members of the Clothing Workers' union. Several housing develop-ments, notably Amalgamated Houses and Co-op City in the Bronx and Amalgamated Dwellings in lower Manhattan, attest to his accomplishments.

**AHEARN PARK** Named in 1923 for State Assemblyman, Senator, and Manhattan Borough President John Francis Ahearn. Ahearn, who had come to power at the turn of the century as part of the Tammany machine, was removed from office under allegations that his office was financially irresponsible. He died in 1920.

*The* Pelican *Sloop of War capturing Allen's* Argus.

**ALLEN STREET** Named in 1817 for U.S. Navy Officer William H. Allen, killed in bat-tle during the War of 1812. The Minutes of the Common Council, in declaring the change of name from 4th Street, pay tribute to Allen who "Commanded the Sloop of War *Argus* of Eighteen Guns, and died of a Wound received on Board of that Vessel when she was engaged with the British Sloop of War *Pelican*."

**A NEW STREET** As in the Financial District, a new street that remains nameless. This one was probably cut through between Baruch Drive and Mangin Street when the Baruch Houses were built in 1954, truncating their routes.

**ATTORNEY STREET** The identity of the attorney or attorneys memorialized in this street name has not been documented. The name, however, may refer to three attorney owners of the land through which the street was laid prior to 1797: Henry Livingston, 1757–1823, who became a justice of the New York and United States Supreme Courts; Morgan Lewis, 1754–1844, chief justice of the New York State Supreme Court; and John Quackenbos.

**BARUCH DRIVE & PLACE**   Named in 1939 for Simon Baruch, 1840–1921, surgeon and philanthropist. Professor of hydrotherapy, Baruch promoted bathing as vital to good health, and was instrumental in the erection in 1891 of the first public bath in the U.S. on Rivington Street. Simon was the father of financier Bernard Baruch, 1870–1965.

*Simon Baruch*

**BIALYSTOKER PLACE/WILLETT STREET**   The street was originally called Willett Street for Marinus Willett, sheriff of New York City in 1784, and mayor for the year 1807. The name Bialystoker Place was added to the street in 1987 to honor the neighborhood's Jewish immigrants from the area of Bialystok, Poland, who founded the Bialystoker Synagogue at No. 7 in 1878.

**BOWERY**   In the 17th century, Dutch farms called "bowerij" were laid out in this part of New Amsterdam along the path of an old Indian trail. Known since that time as the Bowery, the thoroughfare became the first segment of the Post Road from New York City to Boston.

**BROOME STREET**   For John Broome, 1738–1810, prominent Manhattan merchant and lieutenant governor of New York State in 1804.

**CANNON STREET**   For Abraham Cannon, 18th-century baker and tavern keeper. Cannon bought land in the area that had been part of an estate forfeited by James de Lancey, Jr., a Loyalist who resettled in England in the early days of the Revolution.

**CHERRY STREET**   This was originally a lane leading to a cherry orchard belonging to Thomas Delavall, mayor of New York City in 1666, 1670, and 1678.

**CHRYSTIE STREET**   Named in 1817 for Lieutenant Colonel John Chrystie, hero of the War of 1812 who died of illness contracted during that conflict.

**CLINTON STREET**   Henry Rutgers, whose property the street ran through, named it in 1792 for George Clinton with whom Rutgers had led the successful campaign for Thomas Jefferson's presidency. Clinton was governor of New York State from 1777 to 1795 (i.e. first American governor of the state), and 1801 to 1804. He had the distinction of serving as vice president under both Thomas Jefferson and James Madison.

**COLUMBIA STREET**   During the Revolution, the word "Columbia" became popular with rebellious colonists as it associated their creation of a new country with the discovery of the New World by Columbus. This street, laid out prior to 1799, was a proud reference to that earlier adventure.

**CORLEAR'S HOOK PARK**   The area of lower Manhattan Island which juts out into the East River between the Williamsburg and Manhattan Bridges was called Corlear's Hook for the Van Corlear family, early Dutch settlers, who owned the land.

Lower East Side

**DELANCEY STREET** For the family of James de Lancey, Sr., prominent figure in 18th-century New York through whose land the street was cut. De Lancey, 1702–1760, was appointed chief justice of the colonial supreme court of judicature in 1733, in which position he presided over the trial of Peter Zenger, the printer whose acquittal on charges of seditious libel was the first victory for freedom of the press in this country. In 1753 de Lancey was named lieutenant governor of the province. He bought this property in 1744.

*James de Lancey, Sr.*

**EAST BROADWAY** Originally leading to the property of the Rutgers family and previously named Harmon Street for Harmon Rutgers. The street was lengthened to meet the need for a north-south artery east of Broadway in the mid-18th century and the name was changed in 1831 at the request of the street's residents.

**EAST HOUSTON STREET** The eastern portion of the street named for William Houstoun, 1757–1812, of a prominent Georgia family. Houstoun married a daughter of Manhattan landowner Nicholas Bayard III. The Georgia provenance of the name accounts for its pronunciation which distinguishes it from the Texas city. The spelling was altered over time.

**EDUCATIONAL ALLIANCE CORNER** Named in 1989 to recognize the Educational Alliance, formed in 1889 by established German Jews to "Americanize" later-arriving eastern European Jewish immigrants on the Lower East Side. The Educational Alliance building, constructed in 1893, was used for classes to prepare immigrant children for public school, and to teach adults English and civics. The Alliance remains active in the building on this corner.

**ELDRIDGE STREET** Named in 1817 for Lieutenant Joseph C. Eldridge, killed by Canadian Indians during the War of 1812. In enacting the street name, the Minutes of the Common Council declare, "he was arrested in his hopeful Career by the Tomahawk of the Savages in Upper Canada."

**ESSEX STREET** A street named for the English county by 18th-century landowner James de Lancey, Jr., son of James Sr. above, and laid out by him to form the east side of the "Great (or de Lancey) Square" he created on the property inherited from his father. A Loyalist, de Lancey's plans were scuttled by his resettling in England early in the Revolution and forfeiting his estates.

**FORSYTH STREET** Named in 1817 for Lieutenant Colonel Benjamin Forsyth, who died of wounds suffered in the War of 1812.

**FREEMAN ALLEY** Possibly named for Uzal W. Freeman who was appointed city surveyor in 1810. At the time, Freeman lived on the Bowery near Grand Street.

**GOUVERNEUR STREET & SLIP EAST AND WEST**  For Nicholas Gouverneur, respected 18th-century merchant who released the land for the street to the city in 1798.

**GRAND STREET**  This street was laid out by James de Lancey, Jr., son of James Sr. above, to be the drive to his "Great (or de Lancey) Square" (see Essex Street above).

**HAMILTON FISH PARK**  For Hamilton Fish, 1808–1893, New York State governor, senator, and secretary of state under President Ulysses S. Grant.

**HARRY BLUMENSTEIN PLAZA**  Named in 1976 shortly after the death of a beloved police officer who served on the Lower East Side and rose to the rank of deputy inspector.

**HENRY STREET**  For Henry Rutgers, 1745–1830, who owned a large estate in this area and gave land to the city for streets,

*Hamilton Fish*

schools, and churches. The family wealth was based on trade and brewing.

**JACKSON STREET**  For Andrew Jackson, 1767–1845, seventh president of the United States.

**JEFFERSON STREET**  For Thomas Jefferson, 1743–1826, third president of the United States.

**LEWIS STREET**  Two attributions are found: one source cites as the street's namesake Morgan Lewis, 1754–1844, chief justice of the New York State Supreme Court and governor of the state in 1804. The other contends that it was named for Morgan's father, Francis Lewis, an early 18th-century immigrant from Wales. Francis was a fur trader who was elected to the First Continental Congress and signed the Declaration of Independence.

*Thomas Jefferson*

**LUDLOW STREET**  Named in 1817 for Lieutenant Augustus C. Ludlow, naval hero of the War of 1812. Second in command of the American frigate *Chesapeake*, it was to Ludlow that his captain, James Lawrence, being mortally wounded, shouted the famous command, "Don't give up the ship!" Ludlow obeyed until fatally wounded himself.

**MADISON STREET**  For James Madison, 1751–1836, fourth president of the United States.

**MANGIN STREET**  For Joseph Francis Mangin, city surveyor and architect who was appointed chief engineer of fortifications for the city. Along with John McComb he designed the present City Hall, completed in 1811.

**MARTIN R. CELIC PLAZA** Named in 1979 after the death of a fireman, aged 25, who was killed in an arson fire on East 8th Street.

**MONROE STREET** For James Monroe, 1758–1831, fifth president of the United States.

**MONTGOMERY STREET** For Revolutionary War General Richard Montgomery, killed in 1775 in the Battle of Quebec. His last words, reportedly, were, "Men of New York, you will not fear to follow where your general leads!"

**NORFOLK STREET** A street laid out by James de Lancey, Jr. on his property and named for the English county (see Essex Street above).

**ORCHARD STREET** The name arose from the fact that the street ran through orchards on the de Lancey property.

**PITT STREET** For William Pitt, Earl of Chatham, 1708–1778. Pitt was a British statesman greatly admired by the colonists for his stance supporting their right to independence.

**RHEBA LIEBOWITZ SQUARE** Named in 1986 for this Lower East Side community activist who died in 1983.

**RIDGE STREET** The name refers to a hilly ridge on property belonging to the de Lancey family.

*James Rivington's* New-York Gazetteer.

**RIVINGTON STREET** Named by James de Lancey, Jr. for James Rivington, 1724–1802, printer, bookseller, and publisher of the *New-York Gazetteer*, a loyalist journal. Rivington was appointed by de Lancey to help sell his estates after he resettled in England early in the Revolution, though ultimately the land was forfeited.

**RUTGERS STREET & SLIP** For Henry Rutgers, 1745–1830, who owned a large estate in this area and gave land to the city for streets, schools, and churches. The family's wealth was based on trade and brewing.

**SAMUEL A. SPIEGEL SQUARE** Named in 1980 for the judge of the City Civil Court and New York State Supreme Court. As Manhattan assemblyman in the late 1950s and early 1960s, Spiegel was known for sponsoring tenant-friendly legislation.

**SAMUEL DICKSTEIN PLAZA** Named in 1963 for the New York State Supreme Court justice, legislator, and congressman 1885–1954. Dickstein served as chairman of the Immigration and Naturalization Committee and as a member of the Un-American Activities Committee.

**SARA DELANO ROOSEVELT PARK**   Named when the park was opened in 1934 for President Franklin Delano Roosevelt's mother, 1854–1941, a figure greatly respected by residents of the Lower East Side.

**SCHIFF MALL**   Named in 1981 for Jacob Schiff, 1848–1918, head of the banking firm Kuhn, Loeb & Co. A supporter of educational institutions, Schiff donated the building for the Jewish Theological Seminary, and was a founder of Barnard College and Montefiore Hospital.

**SEWARD PARK**   For William Henry Seward, 1801–1872, governor of New York from 1839 to 1842, U.S. senator in 1849, and secretary of state during the Civil War. The park was named in recognition of his support for immigrants.

**SHERIFF STREET**   For Marinus Willett, sheriff of New York City in 1784 and mayor of the city 1807–1808.

**SOUTH STREET**   In the 18th century, landfill extended Manhattan Island into the East River, first past Pearl Street, and later beyond the line of Water Street. Subsequent expansion pushed the shoreline past Front Street, creating a waterfront with South Street running along the river's edge.

**STANTON STREET**   Named by James de Lancey, Jr. for his agent, George Stanton (see Essex Street above).

*William Henry Seward*

**STRAUS SQUARE**   Named in 1931 for Nathan Straus, 1848–1931, a partner in the department store Abraham and Straus and, with his brother Isidor, owner of R. H. Macy. Straus's charitable efforts included the development of a laboratory for pasteurizing milk and its distribution to the needy. In addition, he provided aid to the poor during the depressions of 1894 and 1914–1915.

**SUFFOLK STREET**   A street laid out by James de Lancey, Jr. on his property and named for the English county (see Essex Street above).

**THOMAS A. WYLIE PLACE**   Named in 1996 for a firefighter killed after just three months on the job.

**WATER STREET**   As per the above South Street entry, Water Street was the first new shoreline road created on 18th-century landfill.

**WILLIAM "BILL" SICKLICK PLACE**   Named in 1996 after the death of a local community leader.

# Chinatown

The fact that Chinatown contains only one Asian place name provides a clue to its history. The influx of immigrants from Asia is visibly dominant in this part of town, and yet, relative to other immigrants to the city, their numbers are fewer and the imprint of Asian culture seems to barely overlay what came before. Clearly, Chinatown was not always Asian. Names such as Mott, Bayard, and Baxter, which summon up visions of Asian food markets and restaurants, had nothing at all to do with the culture presently ensconced in these precincts, but belonged, respectively, to pre- and post-Revolutionary merchants of European origin, and a hero of the Mexican War. In the early 19th century small numbers of Chinese sailors and merchants were in evidence in the city. Their numbers exploded with the 1869 completion of the transcontinental railroad which released thousands of Chinese laborers to seek employment elsewhere. It is thought that this neighborhood initially attracted the Asian population due to its relative proximity to the harbor. From its beginnings as a tiny enclave, Chinatown has continuously pushed out of its early bounds. The presence within Chinatown's current limits of a handful of Italian honorary street names, along with a smattering of Italian restaurants bravely holding their own, testifies to the steady expansion of one culture into the vacuum left by another.

**ALLEN STREET** For U.S. Navy officer William H. Allen, killed in battle during the War of 1812. According to the Minutes of the Common Council for March 24, 1817 when the street name was changed from 4th Street, Allen "Commanded the Sloop of War *Argus* of Eighteen Guns, and died of a Wound received on Board of that Vessel when she was engaged with the British Sloop of War *Pelican*."

**ANCIENT ORDER OF HIBERNIANS** This order was founded in nearby St. James Church to aid Irish immigrants arriving in the United States in the 1830s. In 1986, to mark the organization's 150th anniversary, a portion of James Street was named in its honor. The order's current mission is to "keep alive traditions, history and culture of the Irish people," a charge accomplished in part through its sponsorship of the St. Patrick's Day Parade.

**BAXTER STREET** Named in 1853 for Lieutenant Colonel Charles Baxter, a hero of the Mexican War killed at Chapultepec in 1849.

**BAYARD STREET** This street was once part of the southern boundary of the Bayard estate, and was probably named for Colonel Nicholas Bayard, 1644–1709, nephew of Peter Stuyvesant. Bayard served as mayor of New York, and was jailed during Leisler's Rebellion, 1689–1691. He escaped the gallows by bowing to Leisler's demand that he swear allegiance to the cause of Protestant William III over that of the Catholic James II.

**BOWERY** In the 17th century, Dutch farms called "bowerij" were laid out in this part of New Amsterdam along the path of an old Indian trail. Known since that time as the Bowery, the thoroughfare became the first segment of the Post Road from New York City to Boston.

**BROOME STREET**  For John Broome, 1738–1810, prominent merchant and lieutenant governor of New York State in 1804.

**CANAL STREET**  The street was originally a stream that ran from what was once "Fresh Water," or "Collect," Pond, north of present-day City Hall, to the Hudson River. By the early 19th century, in the wake of a yellow fever epidemic, the pond had become seriously polluted and was identified as a health hazard. In 1805, to drain off the pond, the stream was widened into a canal—hence the name—and both were filled in over a decade later.

**CATHERINE STREET & SLIP**  For Catherine DesBrosses, daughter of Jacques (James) DesBrosses, 17th-century Huguenot immigrant whose rum distillery was located near the East River. Catherine was the sister of James and Oliver (below), and of Elias (see TriBeCa).

**CENTRE MARKET PLACE**  Site of one of the official New York City markets, established at Centre and Grand Streets in 1817. Note the British spelling of the name.

**CENTRE STREET**  Originally called Collect Street, this street was laid over the filled-in "Collect," or "Fresh Water," Pond. The street name was changed in 1828 to identify it as terminating at the Centre Market. As above, note the British spelling of the name.

**CHATHAM SQUARE**  For William Pitt, Earl of Chatham, 1708–1778. Pitt was a British statesman greatly admired by the colonists for his stance supporting their right to independence.

**CHERRY STREET**  Originally a lane leading to a cherry orchard belonging to Thomas Delavall, mayor of New York City in 1666, 1670, and 1678.

**CHRYSTIE STREET**  Named in 1817 for Lieutenant Colonel John Chrystie, hero of the War of 1812, who died of illness contracted during that conflict.

**COLUMBUS PARK**  The park was opened as Mulberry Bend Park in 1897. In the 19th century this plot teemed with what reformer and journalist Jacob Riis denounced as the worst tenements in the city. The buildings were demolished under the Tenement House Act of 1895 and replaced with the park. In 1911 an act of the Board of Aldermen changed the park's name in recognition of the fact that it is located where "the first footsteps of our Italian citizens were trod."

*Christopher Columbus*

**DELANCEY STREET** For the family of James de Lancey, Sr., prominent figure in 18th-century New York through whose land the street was cut. De Lancey, 1702–1760, was appointed chief justice of the colonial supreme court of judicature in 1733, in which position he presided over the trial of Peter Zenger, the printer whose acquittal on charges of seditious libel was the first victory for freedom of the press in this country. In 1753 de Lancey was named lieutenant governor of the province. He bought this property in 1744.

**DIVISION STREET** So called as the street marked the boundary line between the Rutgers and the de Lancey farms.

**DOYERS STREET** For Hendrick Doyer, Dutch immigrant who owned property and operated a distillery and tavern in the area at the end of the 18th century.

**EAST BROADWAY** Originally leading to the property of the Rutgers family and named Harmon Street for Harmon Rutgers. The street was lengthened to meet the need for a north-south artery east of Broadway in the mid-18th century and the name was changed in 1831 at the request of the street's residents.

**ELDRIDGE STREET** Named in 1817 for Lieutenant Joseph C. Eldridge, killed by Canadian Indians during the War of 1812. In enacting the street name, the Minutes of the Common Council declare, "he was arrested in his hopeful Career by the Tomahawk of the Savages in Upper Canada."

**ELIZABETH STREET** The street name is shown on maps as early as the mid-18th century adjacent to streets associated with three intermarried families: the Bayards, the Rynderses, and the Leislers. This street's location suggests that it was named for Elizabeth Rynders, wife of Nicholas Bayard II, and daughter of Hester Leisler Rynders.

**ESSEX STREET** A street named for the English county by 18th-century landowner James de Lancey, Jr., son of James Sr. above, and laid out by him to form the east side of the "Great (or de Lancey) Square" he created on the property inherited from his father. A Loyalist, de Lancey's plans were scuttled by his resettling in England early in the Revolution and forfeiting his estates.

**FORSYTH STREET** Named in 1817 for Lieutenant Colonel Benjamin Forsyth, who died of wounds received in the War of 1812.

**FRANK D'AMICO PLAZA** Named in 1984 for an educator who died in 1980, having devoted his career to bettering neighborhood Junior High School 65 (now I.S. 131).

**GRAND STREET** This street was laid out by James de Lancey, Jr., son of James Sr. above, to be the drive to his "Great (or de Lancey) Square" (see Essex Street above).

**HENRY STREET**   For Henry Rutgers, 1745–1830, who owned a large estate in this area and gave land to the city for streets, schools, and churches. The family wealth was based on trading and brewing.

**HESTER STREET**   For Hester Leisler, whose father was Jacob Leisler, self-appointed lieutenant governor of New York, 1689–1691. As a result of the Glorious Revolution in England which overthrew James II in 1688, anti-Catholic Jacob Leisler took command of the province, anticipating that William of Orange would ascend to the British throne. Leisler "père" was later hanged when the forces of King William turned against him. Hester married Benjamin Rynders, a wealthy Dutch settler.

**JAMES STREET**   Named for James DesBrosses, 1705–1781, son of Jacques (James) DesBrosses, 17th-century Huguenot immigrant, whose rum distillery was located near the East River. James was the brother of Catherine and Oliver (above and below), and of Elias (see TriBeCa).

**JOHN J. LAMULA SQUARE**   Named in 1983 for the state assemblyman, a key sponsor of the Alfred E. Smith Houses in Lower Manhattan, and district leader from 1949–1969.

**KENMARE STREET**   Named by Big Tim Sullivan, 1863–1913, for his mother's birthplace in Ireland. Sullivan was a colorful and controversial Lower East Side political leader who championed women's rights, tenement reform, and organized labor.

**KIMLAU SQUARE**   A memorial arch was erected in Chatham Square in 1962 in memory of Lieutenant Benjamin Ralph Kimlau, and in recognition of the participation of the Chinese as our allies in World War II. Kimlau, a former resident of the neighborhood, was a B-25 pilot in the U.S. Army Air Corps. He was shot down over New Guinea in 1944.

**LOUIS F. DESALVIO CORNER**   Named in 1993 for this leader of the Italian-American community. Representing Long Island in the State Assembly for 38 years, he is known for helping to create Off-Track Betting.

**LUDLOW STREET**   Named in 1817 for Lieutenant Augustus C. Ludlow, naval hero of the War of 1812. Second in command of the American frigate *Chesapeake*, it was to Ludlow that his mortally wounded captain, James Lawrence, shouted the famous command, "Don't give up the ship!" Ludlow obeyed until fatally injured himself.

**MADISON STREET**   For James Madison, 1751–1836, fourth president of the United States.

**MARKET STREET & SLIP**   Called George Street until the early 19th century, the name was probably among those changed after the Revolution in an effort to eradicate all place-names reminiscent of British royal figures. The boat slip which once existed at the base of the street was possibly the site of a market such as existed at other slips, a fact which may explain the street's new name.

**MECHANICS ALLEY** Though no documentation exists for the name of this short alley, it may be associated with the early history of the General Society of Mechanics and Tradesmen. Formally founded in 1785 and still in existence today, the Society's original mission was to advance and protect the political and economic interests of American craftsmen. Though their first meeting hall was at Broadway and Park Place, they owned land in the Chatham Square area, giving rise to the speculation that their organization may be the basis for this alley's name.

**MONROE STREET** For James Monroe, 1758–1831, fifth president of the United States.

**MOSCO STREET** Named in 1982 for Lower East Side community activist Frank Mosco who died that year. Mosco was best known for his work on issues of youth problems, housing for low-income families, and the elderly. In 1976, Mosco took a leave of absence as chairman of Community Board No. 3, having been arrested on suspicion of extorting money from an undercover police officer posing as a street vendor near the South Street Seaport.

**MOTHER FRANCIS XAVIER CABRINI TRIANGLE** Named in 1993 for the missionary who emigrated from Italy in 1889 and became a religious leader for Italian immigrants. Cabrini traveled widely in this country and founded 67 educational institutions, orphanages, and hospitals here, in Europe, and in Central and South America. She was the first American citizen to be canonized by the Roman Catholic Church.

**MOTT STREET** For Jacob Mott, a wealthy merchant who served as the city's deputy mayor and as alderman from 1804 to 1810.

**MULBERRY STREET** The name appears on maps as early as the late 18th century, and probably referred to a grove of mulberry trees in the area.

**OLIVER STREET** For Oliver DesBrosses, son of 17th-century Huguenot immigrant Jacques (James) DesBrosses whose rum distillery was located near the East River. Oliver was the brother of Catherine and James (above), and of Elias (see TriBeCa).

**ORCHARD STREET** Named for the fact that it ran through the orchards of the de Lancey family.

**PARK ROW** Originally Chatham Street, but changed in the first quarter of the 19th century presumably to note its path along one side of City Hall Park. City Hall itself was completed in 1811.

**PEARL STREET** Named for the oyster shells left in the area by the native Lenape Indians. Before landfill extended Manhattan Island into the East River in the 18th century, this was the waterfront road.

Chinatown

**PELL STREET**  Thomas Pell received the greater part of what is now Westchester county (hence Pelham) in a grant from British governor Colonel Thomas Dongan at the end of the 17th century. The street is named for his nephew John who inherited his uncle's estate.

**PIKE STREET & SLIP**  For Brigadier General Zebulon Montgomery Pike, 1779–1813, after whom the peak is named. Pike died in battle in Canada during the War of 1812.

**ROBERT F. WAGNER SR. PLACE**  Wagner, 1877–1953, was a German immigrant and politician who was father and grandfather to two other politicians of the same name. Wagner Senior served as state senator in 1908, justice of the New York State Supreme Court from 1918 to 1926, and as U.S. senator in 1926.

*Zebulon Montgomery Pike*

**RUTGERS STREET**  For Henry Rutgers, 1745–1830, who owned a large estate in this area and gave land to the city for streets, schools, and churches. The family's wealth was based on trade and brewing.

**ST. JAMES PLACE**  Formerly New Bowery, this street was renamed in honor of the church built nearby in 1837.

**SARA DELANO ROOSEVELT PARK**  Named when the park was opened in 1934 for President Franklin Delano Roosevelt's mother, 1854–1941, a figure greatly respected by residents of the Lower East Side.

*Sara Delano Roosevelt*

**SCHIFF MALL**  Named in 1981 for Jacob Schiff, 1848–1918, head of the banking firm Kuhn, Loeb & Co. A supporter of educational institutions, Schiff donated the building for the Jewish Theological Seminary, and was a founder of Barnard College and Montefiore Hospital.

**SOUTH STREET**  In the 18th century, landfill extended the shoreline of Manhattan Island into the East River, first past Pearl Street, and later beyond the line of Water Street. Subsequent expansion pushed the shoreline past Front Street, creating a waterfront with South Street running along the river's edge.

**WATER STREET**  As above, Water Street was the first new shoreline road created on 18th-century landfill.

# Little Italy & NoLIta

Historically, newcomers from Italy have settled in neighborhoods populated by immigrants from their home village, if not their home street. Though this meant that Little Italys sprang up in many parts of the metropolitan area, the community in Lower Manhattan was considered the heart of the city's Italian cultural life. In recent decades, Little Italy has dwindled to a shadow of its former self. Once a robust area of restaurants and buzzing sidewalk life, it is being compressed from the south by a spreading Chinatown, and on the north by kicky NoLIta. This diminishment has been facilitated by the emigration of younger generations of Italians to suburban pastures. Interestingly, the "festas" are still a big draw for the recently relocated and the curious. NoLIta, the skinny triangle NOrth of Little ITAly and bounded by Lafayette Street and the Bowery, was once the ne plus ultra of residential zones. The houses erected here in the 1830s and 1840s glowed with wealth newly stimulated by the end of the War of 1812. Typically, this splendor was not to last and, once again, commerce displaced gentility. Until recently nondescript and gritty, these streets are now taking on new life as they sprout antique shops and toney restaurants.

*John Jacob Astor*

**ASTOR PLACE**   For John Jacob Astor, by the 1830s the richest man in America. Astor arrived in the United States in 1784 and worked for his brother selling musical instruments. He went on to achieve enormous success as a trader in furs and goods from the Far East. Astor converted his profits into Manhattan real estate, eventually relinquishing his other interests to deal exclusively in land. He owned a large parcel near what is now Astor Place, hence the beaver on the tile medallions in the Astor Place subway station.

**BLEECKER STREET**   For Anthony Bleecker, a late 18th-century writer who owned the land here and ceded the street to the city in 1809.

**BOND STREET**   Possibly for Captain William Bond, city surveyor in the early 18th century, though a more likely explanation derives from a description of Broadway found in an 1817 guidebook to New York City. Referring to the elegant London street, the author extolled Broadway as "the Bond-Street of New-York." By the early 1830s, Manhattan's Bond Street was indeed a prime address and could well have merited the name.

**BOWERY**   In the 17th century, Dutch farms known as "bowerji" were laid out in this part of New Amsterdam along the path of an old Indian trail. Known since that time as the Bowery, the thoroughfare became the first segment of the Post Road from New York City to Boston.

*Grover Cleveland*

**CLEVELAND PLACE**   For President Grover Cleveland, 1837–1908. Cleveland was mayor of Buffalo in 1881, and governor of New York State in 1882. Cleveland served two terms in the White House, elected in 1884 and again in 1892.

**EAST HOUSTON STREET**   The eastern portion of the street named for William Houstoun, 1757–1812, of a prominent Georgia family, who married a daughter of Manhattan landowner Nicholas Bayard III. The Georgia provenance of the name accounts for its pronunciation which distinguishes it from the Texas city. The spelling was altered over time.

**ELIZABETH STREET**   As early as the mid-18th century, maps show the name of this street in close proximity to other streets associated with three intermarried families: the Bayards, the Rynderses, and the Leislers. The street's location suggests that it may be named for Elizabeth Rynders, wife of Nicholas Bayard II, and daughter of Hester Leisler Rynders.

**GREAT JONES STREET**   Named in 1806 for Samuel Jones, a renowned lawyer and owner of land in this vicinity who died in 1819. The adjective distinguishes this street from the narrower, previously existing, Jones Street in Greenwich Village.

**JERSEY STREET**   According to the Minutes of the Common Council, the street name, formerly Columbia, or Columbian Alley, was changed in 1829 on the petition of "Richard Duryea, Charles H. Hall and others." No reason given.

**KENMARE STREET**   Named by Big Tim Sullivan, 1863–1913, for his mother's birthplace in Ireland. Sullivan was a colorful and controversial Lower East Side political leader who championed women's rights, tenement reform, and organized labor.

**LAFAYETTE STREET**   Named in 1825 by John Jacob Astor, through whose land the street was laid. Astor wished to honor the Marquis de Lafayette, the Revolutionary War hero, who had recently revisited the city.

**LIEUTENANT PETROSINO SQUARE**   Named in 1987 for Lieutenant Joseph Petrosino, a police officer who, when he joined the force in 1883, was the city's shortest officer at 5'3". Disguised as a tunnel worker, a blind beggar, and a gangster, he infiltrated and exposed the criminal gangs that preyed on Italian immigrants. Promoted to detective, he was assigned to uncover anarchists, and warned President McKinley of the danger to his life. Petrosino's warnings were ignored and McKinley was assassinated in 1901. Working in Italy as part of an effort to stamp out the American-Italian mafia connection, Petrosino was shot to death in Palermo in 1909.

Little Italy & NoLIta

65

**MARGARET SANGER SQUARE**  Named in 1993 for the activist and birth control advocate Margaret Sanger, 1879–1966. She was the founder of the organization that became the Planned Parenthood Federation whose New York offices are near this location.

**MOTT STREET**  For Jacob Mott, a wealthy merchant who served as the city's deputy mayor and as alderman from 1804 to 1810.

*Mulberry branch*

**MULBERRY STREET**  The name appears on maps as early as the late 18th century and probably referred to a grove of mulberry trees in the area.

**PRINCE STREET**  Named by the British, it escaped being renamed after the Revolution.

**SHINBONE ALLEY**  The name of this alley, which is indicated by a sign on Lafayette Street (when someone has not "borrowed" it), arose from the shape that it makes in conjunction with Jones Alley across the street.

**SPRING STREET**  Named for the fact that in early New York a spring ran along the path of this street.

# SoHo

The name is an acronym for SOuth of HOuston (Street), a moniker adopted in the 1960s. Farmland until the early 19th century, this section underwent the transformation that Manhattan Island's long, thin shape rendered inevitable in a climate of booming prosperity and growth. As had been the case to the south, and as would soon be the case to the north, the marketplace, following newly opened north-south arteries up the middle of the island, pushed residential enclaves ahead of it. By the first quarter of the 19th century, exclusive shops and elegant homes had installed themselves in these environs. It did not take long, however, for the gentry to feel commerce, and all that it implied in terms of proximity to workplaces and people, nipping at their heels, and to decamp to the next fashionable purlieus just uptown. Commerce in this instance took the form of retail emporia in a new and expansive form made possible and artful by the wonders of cast iron. Nevertheless, even these hulking edifices were left behind in the wake of the relentless march of progress uptown. In the 1960s and '70s, artists, needing cheap, open spaces, stepped in and, spurring an evolution that was soon to be repeated in TriBeCa, turned a near-derelict neighborhood into a vibrant art community. More recently, as artists have been driven out by high rents, SoHo has gone beyond artsy to become a tourist mecca sought out for its trendy shops, restaurants, and the greatest concentration of cast-iron buildings in the world.

**AVENUE OF THE AMERICAS** In 1945, Mayor Fiorello La Guardia added this designation to the name of 6th Avenue to honor the ideals shared by this country and our sister pan-American nations.

**BROADWAY** Originally an Indian trail that ran north from the southern tip of Manhattan, Broadway now extends from the Battery into the Bronx. The street's name derives from its unusual width.

**BROOME STREET** For John Broome, 1738–1810, prominent Manhattan merchant and lieutenant governor of New York State in 1804.

**CANAL STREET** The street was originally a stream that ran from what was once "Fresh Water," or "Collect," Pond, north of present-day City Hall, to the Hudson River. By the early 19th century, in the wake of a yellow fever epidemic, the pond had become seriously polluted and was identified as a health hazard. In 1805, to drain off the pond, the stream was widened into a canal—hence the name—and both were filled in over a decade later.

**CROSBY STREET** For William Bedlow Crosby, philanthropist and great-nephew of Henry Rutgers. Crosby inherited much of Rutgers's land, including his mansion, in 1830. Crosby died in 1865.

**FATHER FAGAN PARK** Named in 1941 for Richard Fagan, 1911–1938, a priest at nearby St. Anthony's Church. Fagan died in a fire in the church rectory when, after escaping, he returned to the building to rescue two other priests. The little plaza also commemorates three firefighters who died in a 1994 fire at 62 Watts Street.

**GRAND STREET** This is the western extension of a street laid out by 18th-century landowner James de Lancey, Jr. It was to lead to the "Great (or de Lancey) Square" de Lancey created on his property in today's Lower East Side before he resettled in England early in the Revolution. De Lancey and other Loyalists forfeited their New York landholdings after the war.

*Fireman from the period when Henry Howard was chief of New York City's volunteer fire department.*

**GREENE STREET** For Revolutionary War General Nathanael Greene, 1742–1786, a Quaker, known for his campaigns in North and South Carolina.

**HOWARD STREET** For Henry Howard, chief of New York City's volunteer fire department from 1857 to 1860. (Firefighting in the city was done on an entirely volunteer basis until 1865.) Howard introduced such improvements as the constant alert and sleeping quarters in fire stations.

**JERSEY STREET** According to the Minutes of the Common Council, the street name, formerly Columbia, or Columbian Alley, was changed in 1829 on the petition of "Richard Duryea, Charles H. Hall and others." No reason given.

**KING STREET** In ceding the street to the city in 1807, Trinity Church named it for Rufus King, 1755–1827, statesman and diplomat. King was appointed to the first U.S. Senate and served a second term in the Senate from 1813 to 1825. He was minister to Britain, and ran, unsuccessfully, for vice president in 1804 and 1808, and for president against James Monroe in 1816.

**LAFAYETTE STREET** Named in 1825 by John Jacob Astor, through whose land the street was laid. Astor wished to honor the Revolutionary War hero, the Marquis de Lafayette, who had recently revisited the city.

**Macdougal Street**    For General Alexander MacDougal, 1733–1786, a founder of the Sons of Liberty, a group of working-class men active in resisting British policies in the colonies before the Revolution. MacDougal went on to become the first president of the Bank of New York and a state senator.

*Alexander MacDougal*

**Mercer Street**    For Revolutionary War Brigadier General Hugh M. Mercer, 1725–1777, killed at the Battle of Princeton.

**Prince Street**    Named by the British, it escaped being renamed after the Revolution.

**Spring Street**    Named for the fact that in early New York a spring ran along the path of this street.

**Sullivan Street**    For Revolutionary War Brigadier General John Sullivan, 1740–1795.

**Thompson Street**    For Revolutionary War Brigadier General William Thompson, who served under General Philip Schuyler in New York and Canada.

**Watts Street**    For merchant John Watts, a founder of the Leake and Watts Orphan Asylum, opened 1830–1831.

**West Broadway**    Though sections of it were originally called by other names, this thoroughfare was extended and unified in the early 19th century to meet the need for a north-south artery west of Broadway.

**West Houston Street**    The western portion of the street named for William Houstoun, 1757–1812, of a prominent Georgia family. Houstoun married a daughter of Manhattan landowner Nicholas Bayard III. The Georgia provenance of the name accounts for its pronunciation which distinguishes it from the Texas city. The spelling was altered over time.

**Wooster Street**    For Revolutionary War General David Wooster, 1711–1777, killed in Danbury, Connecticut, in battle against the British forces under Sir William Howe.

# NoCa

Until this writing, an oddly shaped wedge of the far west side of Manhattan had escaped the vogue for christening newly "discovered" neighborhoods with catchy names. Edged on the west by the Hudson River, and hemmed in by the West Village to the north, SoHo to the east, and TriBeCa to the south—but not quite a part of any of them—may it henceforth be defined by its position NOrth of CAnal (Street). Part of the extensive tract ceded by Queen Anne to Trinity Church in 1705, its 15 minutes of fame occurred during the Revolution when George Washington briefly used Richmond Hill, a mansion located here, as his headquarters. John Jacob Astor, who bought Richmond Hill in 1803, profited from the development of the estate into blocks and lots which still boast some of the city's most charming and well-preserved Federal-style row houses. By the late 19th century the bulk of shipping activity had migrated from the shallower East River to the Hudson and the shoreline here bristled with piers. Businesses involved in the transporting of goods by ship and train, along with markets, breweries, and a sugar refinery, filled the bustling riverfront blocks. In the last quarter century, with the Hudson piers unable to handle containerized cargo, large-scale shipping has shifted to New Jersey, leaving printing, the area's other traditional industry, to grapple with the transition to the cyber word. A multiple-personality locale, NoCa is on its way to becoming the next darling of the café set.

**AVENUE OF THE AMERICAS** In 1945, Mayor Fiorello La Guardia added this designation to the name of 6th Avenue to honor the ideals shared by this country and our sister pan-American nations.

**BROOME STREET** For John Broome, 1738–1810, prominent Manhattan merchant and lieutenant governor of New York State in 1804.

**CANAL STREET** The street was originally a stream that ran from what was once "Fresh Water," or "Collect," Pond, north of present-day City Hall, to the Hudson River. By the early 19th century, in the wake of a yellow fever epidemic, the pond had become seriously polluted and was identified as a health hazard. In 1805, to drain off the pond, the stream was widened into a canal—hence the name—and both were filled in over a decade later.

**CHARLTON STREET** In ceding the street to the city in 1807, Trinity Church named it for Dr. John Charlton, a British surgeon who came here with the British army in 1762. Charlton became statesman John Jay's family doctor.

**DOMINICK STREET** For George Dominick, a Huguenot refugee who arrived here in the mid-18th century and was a vestryman of Trinity Church.

**DUARTE SQUARE** For Joan Pablo Duarte, 1813–1876, founder of the Dominican Republic. The statue of Duarte in this square is one of six statues of Latin American leaders along the Avenue of the Americas.

**GRAND STREET** This is the western extension of a street laid out by 18th-century landowner James de Lancey, Jr. It was to lead to the "Great (or de Lancey) Square" de Lancey created on his property on today's Lower East Side before he resettled in England early in the Revolution. De Lancey and other Loyalists forfeited their New York landholdings after the War.

**GREENWICH STREET** One of the earliest roads to run from the Battery to 14th Street, it was named for the village to which it led. The street was created on landfill carried out intermittently from 1739 to 1785.

**HUDSON RIVER PARK** The area between the Joe DiMaggio Highway and the Hudson River which is being developed as parkland from Chambers Street to 59th Street.

**HUDSON STREET** Named for the fact that it parallels the river nearby.

**KING STREET** In ceding the street to the city in 1807, Trinity Church named it for Rufus King, 1755–1827, statesman and diplomat. King was appointed to the first U.S. Senate and served a second term in the Senate from 1813 to 1825. He was minister to Britain and ran, unsuccessfully, for vice president in 1804 and 1808, and for president against James Monroe in 1816.

**RENWICK STREET** For James Renwick, 1792–1863, author, engineer, scientist, water-colorist, and teacher. Renwick, whose son James, 1818–1895, was the architect of St. Patrick's Cathedral and Grace Church, was Professor of Natural and Experimental Philosophy and Chemistry at Columbia College, and Trustee of the College.

**SOHO SQUARE** Named for the area it abuts, the square features a statue of Uruguayan independence leader and national hero General Jose Artigas, 1764–1850. It is one of the six statues of Latin American leaders along Avenue of the Americas.

**SPRING STREET** Named for the fact that in early New York a spring ran along the path of this street.

**VANDAM STREET** Another street named by Trinity Church in ceding the street to the city in 1807. Anthony Van Dam, who died that year, was a wine and liquor dealer active in civic affairs.

**VARICK STREET** For Colonel Richard Varick, George Washington's secretary and later city recorder. Varick was appointed mayor of the city by Governor George Clinton in 1789.

WASHINGTON STREET   For President George Washington, 1732–1799.

WATTS STREET   For merchant John Watts, a founder of the Leake and Watts Orphan Asylum, opened 1830–1831.

WEST HOUSTON STREET   The western portion of the street named for William Houstoun, 1757–1812, of a prominent Georgia family. Houstoun married a daughter of Manhattan landowner Nicholas Bayard III. The Georgia provenance of the name accounts for its pronunciation which distinguishes it from the Texas city. The spelling was altered over time.

WEST STREET   Built on 18th-century landfill, this street was named in the certainty that no thoroughfare would exist farther west.

# The Villages

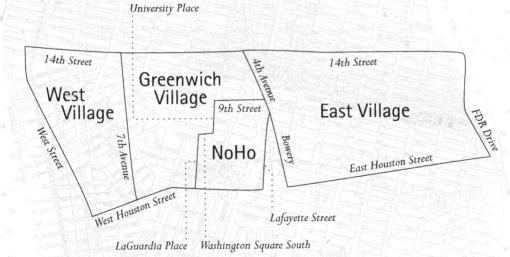

# East Village

The boundaries of the East Village coincide roughly with the farms, or "bowerji," owned in the latter part of the 17th century by Peter Stuyvesant, the last Dutch governor of New Netherland. In the early 19th century, prodded uptown by advancing development, an affluent citizenry made their homes in Federal-style row houses, some of which still bear testimony to a gracious past in the streets around St. Mark's Church in the Bowery. Since that time, the East Village has been a revolving door for ethnicities and nationalities who have used it as a way station between the Lower East Side to the south and their next destination uptown or out of town. Germans, Ukrainians, Italians, eastern European Jews, Latinos, and Asians have all left their marks. The neighborhood earned its "village" title in the mid-20th century as high rents and gentrification squeezed artists, musicians, and intellectuals east from Greenwich Village. Physically, the district is now characterized by large housing developments to the east, countless

community gardens on nearly every street, and a funky, hip/chic

scene of shops and restaurants in the remaining row houses on

its west side. The area residents continue to display an impres-

sive cultural, social, and economic diversity.

**ABE LEBWOHL PARK** Named in 1997 for the Ukrainian immigrant who developed the 2nd Avenue Deli at 2nd Avenue and 10th Street into a New York institution. A beloved and humanitarian neighborhood figure, he was shot and killed in a robbery in 1996.

**ASTOR PLACE** For John Jacob Astor, by the 1830s the richest man in America. Astor arrived in the United States in 1784 and worked for his brother selling musical instruments. He went on to achieve enormous success as a trader in furs and goods from the Far East. Astor converted his profits into Manhattan real estate, eventually relinquishing his other interests to deal exclusively in land. He owned a large parcel near what is now Astor Place, hence the beaver on the tile medallions in the Astor Place subway station.

**AVENUES A, B, C & D** In 1807, the State Legislature appointed a commission to lay out a plan for the orderly expansion of Manhattan Island. The grid plan which the commissioners proposed provided for north-south avenues and east-west streets from approximately Houston Street to Washington Heights. The long avenues that extended to Harlem were numbered. East of 1st Avenue, the short north-south arteries were lettered from A to D.

*Charlie Parker*

**BOWERY** In the 17th century, Dutch farms called "bowerij" were laid out in this part of New Amsterdam along the path of an old Indian trail. Known since that time as the Bowery, the thoroughfare became the first segment of the Post Road from New York City to Boston.

**CHARLIE PARKER PLACE** Named in 1992 for the composer and alto saxophonist who was a founder of bebop. Parker lived in the neighborhood, and died in 1955 at age 35.

**COOPER SQUARE**  For Peter Cooper, 1791–1883, inventor and industrialist who built the first working steam engine and was instrumental in the development of the American iron and cable industries. In 1857–1859, Cooper founded the Cooper Union at this location to provide free education in science, engineering, and art.

*Peter Cooper*

**EAST HOUSTON STREET**  The eastern portion of the street named for William Houstoun, 1757–1812, of a prominent Georgia family. Houston married a daughter of Manhattan landowner Nicholas Bayard III. The Georgia provenance of the name accounts for its pronunciation which distinguishes it from the Texas city. The spelling was altered over time.

**FATHER MANCINI CORNER**  Named in 1989 for the priest who was pastor of the Mary Help of Christians parish on 12th Street for 32 years.

**GUSTAVE HARTMAN SQUARE**  Named in 1936 for the Municipal Court justice active in the 1920s and '30s. As part of his involvement in Jewish philanthropy, Hartman founded the Israel Orphan Asylum.

**LASALLE ACADEMY PLACE**  For the Catholic High School of this name on 2nd Street. Saint Jean Baptiste de la Salle, 1651–1719, founded the Institute of Brothers of the Christian Schools, a teaching order devoted to educating boys.

**LIZ CHRISTY GARDEN**  Founded in 1993 by Liz Christy and the Green Guerrillas, this is the city's original community garden.

**LOISAIDA AVENUE**  Named in 1987 in recognition of the community's Hispanic character. "Loisaida" is the phonetic spelling of the area's name (Lower East Side) as spoken by its Latino population.

**PERETZ SQUARE**  Named in 1952 for noted Yiddish writer I. L. (or J. L. depending on the source) Peretz, 1852–1915, dubbed the "Great Educator" of the Jewish masses.

**ST. MARK'S PLACE**  Named for St. Mark's Church in the Bowery on 10th Street which is the site of the family chapel constructed for Peter Stuyvesant, 1610–1672, the last Dutch governor of New Netherland. Stuyvesant is buried in the churchyard.

**STUYVESANT STREET**  Along with the Bowery, this is the only street surviving from the original street plan on Peter Stuyvesant's land. Used as the driveway from the Bowery to Stuyvesant's property, it is also the only street in the city to run a true east-west course, its odd angle being respected and retained, despite the grid plan, because it led to a church.

**SZOLD PLACE**  Named in 1951 for Henrietta Szold, who founded Hadassah, the Women's Zionist Organization of America, in 1912.

**TARAS SHEVCHENKO PLACE**  Named in 1978 for the Ukrainian painter, poet, novelist, and social reformer who lived from 1814 to 1861.

**TOMPKINS SQUARE & PARK**  For Daniel D. Tompkins, 1774–1825, governor of New York State, 1807–1817, and vice president under James Monroe, 1817–1825. Tompkins owned the land that encompassed the park.

*St. Mark's Church*

# NoHo

Taking its name from its position NOrth of HOuston (Street), NoHo is a recent addition to the pantheon of trendy neighborhood names. Like NoCa, this was a non-distinct area that didn't really belong to any of those on its periphery. Like NoLIta to its east and SoHo to its south, NoHo's commercial palaces uprooted an earlier milieu of patrician gentility. The 19th-century loft buildings so prevalent here once hosted the center of the city's textile industry. Though NoHo's identity has lately emerged through a new appreciation of its architectural heritage, it is an area of vastly mixed use, ranging from such institutions as New York University and the Public Theater, to gyms and a hodgepodge of retail establishments. Resistant to ready categorizing, NoHo's wide-reaching and complex diversity may be this neighborhood's most defining feature.

ASTOR PLACE   For John Jacob Astor, by the 1830s, the richest man in this country. Astor arrived in the United States in 1784 and worked for his brother selling musical instruments. He went on to enormous success as a trader in furs and goods from the Far East. Astor converted his profits into Manhattan real estate, eventually relinquishing his other interests to deal exclusively in land. He owned a large parcel near what is now Astor Place, hence the beaver on the tile medallions in the Astor Place subway station.

BLEECKER STREET   For Anthony Bleecker, a late 18th-century writer who owned the land here and ceded the street to the city in 1809.

BOND STREET   Possibly for Captain William Bond, city surveyor in the early 18th century, though a more likely explanation derives from a description of Broadway found in an 1817 guidebook to New York City. Referring to the elegant London street, the author extolled Broadway as "the Bond-Street of New-York." By the 1830s, Manhattan's Bond Street was indeed a prime address, and could well have merited the name.

BROADWAY   Originally an Indian trail that ran north from the southern tip of Manhattan, Broadway now extends from the Battery into the Bronx. The street's name derives from its unusual width.

CROSBY STREET   For William Bedlow Crosby, philanthropist and great-nephew of Henry Rutgers. Crosby inherited much of Rutgers's land, including his mansion, in 1830. Crosby died in 1865.

EAST & WEST HOUSTON STREET   The eastern and western portions of this street converge at the southern edge of Noho. William Houstoun, 1757–1812, of a prominent Georgia family, married a daughter of Manhattan landowner Nicholas Bayard III. The Georgia provenance of the name accounts for its pronunciation which distinguishes it from the Texas city. The spelling was altered over time.

GREAT JONES STREET & ALLEY   Named in 1806 for Samuel Jones, a renowned lawyer and owner of land in this vicinity who died in 1819. The adjective distinguishes this street from the narrower, previously existing Jones Street in Greenwich Village. As of this writing there was no street sign identifying the Alley which is an extension of Shinbone and Jones Alleys. It runs between and parallel to Broadway and Lafayette Streets, from just south of Bond Street to just north of Great Jones Street.

GREENE STREET   For Revolutionary War hero Nathanael Greene, 1742–1786, a Quaker, noted for his campaigns in North and South Carolina.

JONES ALLEY   A section of Great Jones and Shinbone Alleys.

LAFAYETTE STREET   Named in 1825 by John Jacob Astor, through whose land the street was laid. Astor wished to honor the Revolutionary War hero, the Marquis de Lafayette, who had recently revisited the city.

**LA GUARDIA PLACE**   Named in 1967 in memory of Mayor Fiorello La Guardia who had died 20 years earlier. La Guardia was the city's first Italian mayor.

**MERCER STREET**   For Revolutionary War Brigadier General Hugh M. Mercer, 1725–1777, killed at the Battle of Princeton.

**TIME LANDSCAPE**   Created in 1978 by landscape artist Alan Sonfist to commemorate and replicate on a small scale the forests which once covered Manhattan. The plantings in the 25' x 40' plot are native to the island and grew here before European colonization.

*Fiorello La Guardia*

**UNIVERSITY PLACE**   Named in recognition of adjacent New York University which erected its first building here in 1837.

**WASHINGTON SQUARE, PARK & PLACE**   For President George Washington, 1732–1799. In the late 18th century, the open area here was used as a common burial ground. Converted to a park in 1827, the streets on its perimeter attracted the gentry from the less salubrious precincts downtown. The Greek Revival houses on the north side of the square are eloquent reminders of this gracious architectural moment.

**WAVERLY PLACE**   Sir Walter Scott's death in 1832 prompted area residents to petition to change Factory Street to Waverly Place in commemoration of Scott's popular 1814 novel, *Waverley*. The second "e" was dropped from the spelling of the name.

# Greenwich Village

In the 18th century Greenwich (the "Village" was added later), was a summer retreat for businessmen and their families seeking relief from the hubbub and heat of the city several miles to the south. Sir Peter Warren, vice admiral of the British navy and commander of its fleet in New York, was among the large landholders in the area in the 1740s. Development accelerated as epidemics of cholera and yellow fever in the late 18th and early 19th centuries drove many downtown residents and businesses to seek healthier surroundings in the village. Merchant-class row houses sprouted along the village lanes and a year-round community thrived. Due to residents' efforts to protect and retain it, the irregular street layout survived the 1811 Commissioners' grid plan which divided Manhattan into marketable blocks and lots up to 155th Street. By the beginning of the 20th century, the Village was acquiring a diverse ethnic, economic and political population, known for its tolerance of

alternate lifestyles and support for the arts. It is usually assumed

that Sir Peter, being a navy man, christened the area for the

borough of London through which the prime meridian runs.

The name, however, is said to have predated Warren's arrival

here, and to have been associated with a Dutch farm in the area

called Greenwjck, meaning green inlet or cove.

**AVENUE OF THE AMERICAS**   In 1945, Mayor Fiorello La Guardia added this designation to the name of 6th Avenue to honor the ideals shared by this country and our sister pan-American nations.

**BARROW STREET**   For Thomas Barrow, a vestryman of Trinity Church from 1790 to 1820, and an artist known for his 1807 sketch of the first Trinity Church in ruins after the Great Fire of 1776. Trinity Church ceded the street to the city in 1807, stipulating that it be named for Barrow.

**BEDFORD STREET**   Probably named after the street in London.

**BLEECKER STREET**   For Anthony Bleecker, a late 18th-century writer who owned the land here and ceded the street to the city in 1809.

**BROADWAY**   Originally an Indian trail that ran north from the southern tip of Manhattan, Broadway now extends from the Battery into the Bronx. The street's name derives from its unusual width.

**CARMINE STREET**   No clear attribution for the name of this street is available. Some say that Carmine is a misspelling of the original name, but sources differ as to what that name was. One possibility is Germain, for Lord George Germain, a British secretary of state involved in the treacherous scheme of Benedict Arnold. Another is Carman, after Nicholas Carman, a vestryman of Trinity Church.

**CHARLES STREET** For Charles Christopher Amos, heir of one of the trustees of Sir Peter Warren's Greenwich Village estate. Charles Street runs through the part of Warren's estate inherited by Amos.

**CHRISTOPHER STREET & PARK** Also for the above Charles Christopher Amos through whose inherited parcel this street was laid. There was an Amos Street; it is now West 10th Street.

**CHRISTOPHER STREET/STONEWALL PLACE** Named in 1989 in recognition of the 1969 Stonewall Rebellion which took place at the Stonewall Inn, a gay bar on this block. The event is considered the birth of the gay pride movement.

**CORNELIA STREET** As with other female first-name streets, it is supposed that this street's namesake was the daughter or wife of the real estate developer or landowner through whose property the street was laid. In this instance, among those credited with being the muse is Cornelia Rutgers, daughter of Anthony Rutgers, and wife of a Daniel Leroy. Other contenders include her daughter or Cornelia Haring (Herring), second wife of Samuel Jones, the late 18th– early 19th-century jurist after whom Great Jones Street was named.

**DOWNING STREET** Like Bedford Street above, probably named for the street in London.

**FATHER DEMO SQUARE** For the pastor of the Church of Our Lady of Pompeii who died in 1936 having served for 35 years. The church was started for Italian immigrants by the Fathers of St. Charles and was originally located on Waverly Place.

**GAY STREET** For Sidney Howard Gay, 1814–1888, mid-19th-century managing director of the *New York Tribune*.

**GREENWICH AVENUE** Formerly Greenwich Lane, the avenue was part of the inland road to Greenwich Village, connecting it with the Bowery.

**GROVE STREET** So named because of a grove of trees planted there in the early 19th century.

**JEFFERSON MARKET GARDENS** Named for the market which was here from 1833 to 1929.

**JONES STREET** For the physician Gardiner Jones who ceded the land for the street to the city in 1805.

**LA GUARDIA PLACE** Named in 1967 in memory of Mayor Fiorello La Guardia who had died 20 years earlier. La Guardia was the city's first Italian mayor.

**LEROY STREET** In ceding the street to the city in 1807, Trinity Church named it for Alderman Jacob Leroy, a successful merchant of the first quarter of the 19th century.

**LITTLE RED SQUARE**   The plaza adjacent to the Little Red School House, a private day school, located at Bleecker and 6th Avenue.

**MACDOUGAL STREET & ALLEY**   For General Alexander MacDougal, 1733–1786, a founder of the Sons of Liberty, a group of working-class men active in resisting British policies in the colonies before the Revolution. MacDougal went on to become the first president of the Bank of New York and a state senator. The alley is said to have provided access to the stables and rear entrances of the mansions on Washington Square North.

**MCCARTHY SQUARE**   Named in 1943 for Private First Class Bernard Joseph McCarthy, a native of Greenwich Village who was killed at Guadalcanal, becoming the first local resident to die in World War II.

**MILLIGAN PLACE**   For Samuel Milligan, original owner of this cul-de-sac. Milligan built the houses here in 1852 as accommodations for the workers at a hotel on 5th Avenue.

**MINETTA STREET & LANE**   The lane and street are named for the stream that once ran along their paths. The stream's name is Dutch for "little one."

**MORTON STREET**   For General Jacob Morton, longtime commandant of the New York militia who died in 1836. Trinity Church ceded the land for the street to the city in 1808, stipulating that it be named for the general.

**MULRY SQUARE**   Named in 1920 to honor financier Thomas M. Mulry who died in 1916. Mulry was longtime president of the Emigrant Industrial Savings Bank and a tireless contributor to Catholic charitable causes, in particular the Society of St. Vincent de Paul of which he served as president. Mulry lived nearby on Greenwich Avenue.

**PATCHIN PLACE**   For Aaron Patchin, surveyor for, and son-in-law (some say grandson-in-law) of, Samuel Milligan, above. Built earlier than Milligan Place in 1848, the little byway also housed hotel workers.

**PERRY STREET**   Named in 1813 to honor Commodore Oliver H. Perry, hero of the Battle of Lake Erie in the War of 1812.

**RUTH E. WITTENBERG TRIANGLE**   Named in 1990 for this labor and environmental activist who served on Community Board No. 2 for 40 years.

**SHERIDAN SQUARE**   For Civil War General Philip Henry Sheridan, 1831–1888, known for his victories against the South in Virginia's Shenandoah Valley. Following this combat, Sheridan won renown in the frontier Indian Wars.

**SULLIVAN STREET**   For Revolutionary War Brigadier General John Sullivan, 1740–1795.

*New York University
and Washington
Square, ca. 1850*

**THOMPSON STREET** For Revolutionary War Brigadier General William Thompson who served under General Philip Schuyler in New York and Canada.

**UNIVERSITY PLACE** Named in recognition of adjacent New York University which erected its first building here in 1837.

**VARICK STREET** For Colonel Richard Varick, George Washington's secretary and later city recorder. Varick was appointed mayor of the city by Governor George Clinton in 1789.

**WANAMAKER PLACE** For the first Wanamaker's department store opened at 9th Street and Broadway in 1896.

**WASHINGTON SQUARE, PARK, PLACE & MEWS** All named for George Washington, 1732–1799. In the late 18th century, the open area here was used as a common burial ground. Converted to a park in 1827, the streets on its perimeter attracted the gentry from the less salubrious precincts downtown. The Greek Revival houses on the north side of the square are eloquent reminders of this gracious architectural moment. The Mews were stables and carriage houses for the residences on the Square.

**WAVERLY PLACE** Sir Walter Scott's death in 1832 prompted area residents to petition to change Factory Street to Waverly Place in commemoration of Scott's popular 1814 novel, *Waverley*. The second "e" was dropped from the spelling of the name.

**WES JOICE CORNER** Named in 1999 for the proprietor of the Lion's Head, a well-known literary hangout on Christopher Street. Joice died in 1997.

**WEST HOUSTON STREET** The western portion of the street named for William Houstoun, 1757–1812, of a prominent Georgia family. Houstoun married a daughter of Manhattan landowner Nicholas Bayard III. The Georgia provenance of the name accounts for its pronunciation which distinguishes it from the Texas city. The spelling was altered over time.

Greenwich Village

# West Village

The history of the West Village is confluent with that of NoCa and Greenwich Village above. Like those sections, the West Village was a haven from the periodically disease-ridden nether reaches of the city in the early 19th century. Like NoCa, a portion of the area had been part of Trinity Church's vast holdings. Also like NoCa, by the mid-19th century its western flank was abuzz with markets such as those on Washington, Gansevoort, and Weehawken Streets, and the river front teemed with railroad/shipping activity. This activity was supported by and supplied all manner of noxious land uses such as lime depots, turpentine factories, beef and pork inspection stations, soap works, and breweries. It is no wonder that New Yorkers with residential choices sought the central spine of the island for their homes. Remnants of these genteel purlieus continue to delight the eye as they grace otherwise undistinguished blocks. Along with its neighboring areas, the West Village escaped the imposition of the

Commissioners' Plan of 1811, retaining its own quirky street

arrangement which allows West 4th Street to cross West 10th.

Today the residential blocks retain their old-world charm, and

the waterfront basks in a resurgence as the Francophile crowd

flock to oh-so-authentic West Village bistros.

**ABINGDON SQUARE** For a daughter of Sir Peter Warren, a major 18th-century landowner in the area of Greenwich ("Village" would be added later). Each of Warren's three daughters married well. When Warren's estate was broken up in 1787, daughter Charlotte, who had become the Countess of Abingdon, received a portion of the property that included this parcel. It was acquired by the city in the early 19th century. Though tainted with British aristocratic associations, Charlotte's husband's name survived the post-Revolution purge of other such names.

**BANK STREET** When yellow fever struck the city beginning in the late 18th century, those who could do so fled north to the more salubrious air of Greenwich Village—at the time a small enclave totally separate from the city some two miles to the south. As the epidemics attacked with alarming frequency, even businesses, including banks, a customs house, and newspapers opened branches here. Bank Street's identity was a result of the grouping of several bank offices on one street.

**BARROW STREET** For Thomas Barrow, a vestryman of Trinity Church from 1790 to 1820, and an artist known for his 1807 sketch of the first Trinity Church in ruins after the Great Fire of 1776. Trinity Church ceded the street to the city in 1807, stipulating that it be named for Barrow.

**BEDFORD STREET** Probably named after the street in London.

**BETHUNE STREET** For Mrs. Joanna Bethune, 1770–1860, organizer of the New York Orphan Asylum Society which opened in 1806.

**BLEECKER STREET** For Anthony Bleecker, a late 18th-century writer who owned the land here and ceded the street to the city in 1809.

**BLOOMFIELD STREET**   Named in 1873 for Brigadier General Joseph Bloomfield, commander of the troops and defenses in and near New York harbor during the War of 1812.

**CHARLES STREET & LANE**   For Charles Christopher Amos, heir of one of the trustees of Sir Peter Warren's Greenwich Village estate. Charles Street runs through the part of Warren's estate inherited by Amos.

**CHRISTOPHER STREET**   Also for the above Charles Christopher Amos through whose inherited parcel this street was laid. There was an Amos Street; it is now West 10th Street.

**CLARKSON STREET**   For General Matthew Clarkson, aide-de-camp to Benedict Arnold. Trinity Church ceded the land for the street to the city in 1808, stipulating that it be named for the general.

**COMMERCE STREET**   Like Bank Street, this one got its name during an early 19th-century yellow fever epidemic when many businesses from downtown moved to the Village.

**GANSEVOORT STREET**   For General Peter Gansevoort, one of George Washington's officers. A fort constructed here during the War of 1812 and named for Gansevoort gave the street its name. Gansevoort was the grandfather of author Herman Melville who supported himself for 20 years working as a U.S. customs inspector on the Gansevoort docks which replaced the fort.

**GREENWICH AVENUE**   Formerly Greenwich Lane, the avenue was part of the inland road to Greenwich Village, connecting it with the Bowery.

**GREENWICH STREET**   One of the earliest roads to run from the Battery to 14th Street, it was named for the village to which it led. The street was created on landfill carried out intermittently from 1739 to 1785.

**GROVE STREET**   So named because of a grove of trees planted there in the early 19th century.

**HORATIO STREET**   For Major General Horatio Gates, 1728(?)–1806, of Revolutionary War fame. Gates led the rebel forces in their first major victory of the Revolution which was over General Burgoyne at Saratoga.

**HUDSON RIVER PARK**   The area between the Joe DiMaggio Highway and the Hudson River which is being developed as parkland from Chambers Street to 59th Street.

**HUDSON STREET**   Named for the fact that it parallels the river nearby.

**JACKSON SQUARE**   Probably named for President Andrew Jackson, 1767–1845, this is one of the city's oldest parks.

**JAMES J. WALKER PARK**   This space was a Trinity Church cemetery from 1812 to 1895 when the land was acquired by the city. It was called Hudson Park until renamed in 1947 for the flamboyant song-writer/lawyer who served as mayor of New York City from 1925 to 1932, and whose family had lived on adjacent St. Luke's Place.

*James J. Walker*

**JANE STREET**   Opinions vary as to whether this street was named for a Mr. Jaynes who lived here in the 1750s, or for the wife of a Dutchman who named a path on his property for her.

**LEROY STREET**   In ceding the street to the city in 1807, Trinity Church named it for Alderman Jacob Leroy, a successful merchant of the first quarter of the 19th century.

**MAX GORDON CORNER**   Named in 1996 for the Lithuanian immigrant who opened the first Village Vanguard nightclub on Charles Street in 1934. Revered for Gordon's support of avant-garde jazz, the club later moved to 7th Avenue near 11th Street.

**MORTON STREET**   For General Jacob Morton, longtime commandant of the New York militia who died in 1836. Trinity Church ceded the land for the street to the city in 1808, stipulating that it be named for the general.

**PERRY STREET**   Named in 1813 to honor Commodore Oliver H. Perry, hero of the Battle of Lake Erie in the War of 1812.

**REGGIE FITZGERALD TRIANGLE**   Named in 1997 for the local community leader who died in 1995.

**ST. LUKE'S PLACE**   Named for the nearby church, originally called St. Luke's in the Fields, built as a parish church of Trinity Church in 1822.

**ST. VINCENT'S SQUARE**   Named in 1982 in recognition of the hospital.

**WASHINGTON STREET**   For President George Washington, 1732–1799.

**WAVERLY PLACE**   Sir Walter Scott's death in 1832 prompted area residents to petition to change Factory Street to Waverly Place in commemoration of Scott's popular 1814 novel, *Waverley*. The second "e" was dropped from the spelling of the name.

**WEEHAWKEN STREET**   A produce market where farmers from Weehawken, New Jersey, sold their wares was located here from 1834 to 1844. The Hoboken ferry terminal was nearby.

**WEST HOUSTON STREET**   The western portion of the street named for William Houstoun, 1757–1812, of a prominent Georgia family. Houstoun married a daughter of Manhattan landowner Nicholas Bayard III. The Georgia provenance of the name accounts for its pronunciation which distinguishes it from the Texas city. The spelling was altered over time.

*Waverley author Sir Walter Scott*

**WEST STREET**   Built on 18th-century landfill, this street was named in the certainty that no thoroughfare would exist farther west.

# Midtown South

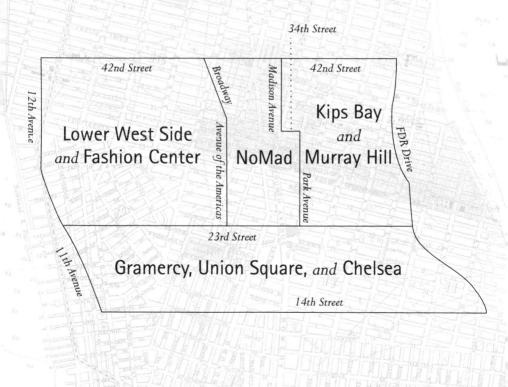

# Gramercy, Union Square & Chelsea

These three sections are treated together here as they have more in common with each other than with the sections around them. Though their expanse encompasses a river-to-river swath of Manhattan that is mostly residential on its eastern flank and mostly commercial on the west, in the 1830s each was being developed from farmland and planned around a square. The Gramercy area—once part of Peter Stuyvesant's bowery—was bought in 1831 by developer Samuel Ruggles who sold lots to affluent families. The surviving elegant row houses attest to the refined company that hobnobbed in the environs of the square. The area declined somewhat during the Depression, but did not suffer the commercial onslaught wrought on its neighbor to the west. Union Square, an awkward triangle resulting from the imposition of the gridiron street plan on the preexisting juncture of Broadway and the Bowery, became a park in 1831. Around it clustered elegant houses and entertainment venues which lasted only until the close of the century when commercial interests pushed their way into the surrounding blocks. In the 20th century, refined shopping migrated north, leaving the square and its surroundings to tacky, low-rent outlets which are just now being chased out themselves by higher-end national chains. Chelsea too was a planned enclave. In the mid-18th century, Captain Thomas Clarke acquired much of the acreage west of 8th Avenue from about 20th to 28th Streets and named it to recall London's bucolic Chelsea Royal Hospital. Inheriting and adding to the property in 1813, Clarke's grandson, Clement Clarke Moore (see the park by that name below), entered the development stakes in progress to the east and went so far as to dictate building styles and materials to the upper-middle-class buyers of his lots. As with other sections of town flanking the Hudson, shipping and trade—in this case, lumber, breweries, and the like—inexorably swallowed the western edges, sending their tentacles through Moore's carefully conceived quarter. Nonetheless, many stately blocks remain, and those less picturesque are being revitalized by the recent arrival from the south of the hippest art gallery scene and the ultra-modern Chelsea Piers sports complex.

**AVENUES A, B & C**  In 1807, the state legislature appointed a commission to lay out a plan for the orderly expansion of Manhattan Island. The grid plan which the commissioners proposed provided for north-south avenues and east-west streets from approximately Houston Street to Washington Heights. The long avenues that extended to Harlem were numbered. East of 1st Avenue, the short north-south arteries were lettered from A to D.

**AVENUE OF THE AMERICAS**  In 1945, Mayor Fiorello La Guardia added this designation to the name of 6th Avenue to honor the ideals shared by this country and our sister pan-American nations.

**BROADWAY**  Originally an Indian trail that ran north from the southern tip of Manhattan, Broadway now extends from the Battery into the Bronx. The street's name derives from its unusual width.

**CHELSEA WATERSIDE PARK**  A portion of the Hudson River Park (see below) in the neighborhood of Chelsea Piers which is slated to span an area both east and west of the Joe DiMaggio Highway from 22nd to 24th Streets.

**CLEMENT CLARKE MOORE PARK**  The City Council record of the 1969 naming of the park declares that the namesake was a "well known poet and clergyman, symbol of New York of yesterday." There is some debate as to whether Moore was a clergyman. What is certain is that this owner of a sizeable portion of land in the neighborhood donated acreage for the General Theological Seminary and taught languages there. Also beyond dispute is that he was the author of the famous poem *'Twas the Night Before Christmas*.

**CUS D'AMATO WAY**  For the boxing instructor at Gramercy Gym who counted among his students Floyd Patterson, Jose Torres, and Mike Tyson. D'Amato died in 1985 having earned a reputation for teaching responsibility and individuality in addition to pugilistic skills.

**DVORAK PLACE** The Czech composer Antonin Dvorak, 1841–1904, came to New York City in 1892 to be the director of the National Conservatory of Music. While holding this position he lived at 327 East 17th Street.

*Mahatma Gandhi*

**GANDHI GARDEN** The statue of Mahatma Gandhi, 1869–1948, Indian nationalist, pacifist, and spiritual leader, was installed at the traffic island near Union Square in 1986.

**GRAMERCY PARK** "Gramercy" is an anglicizing of the area's Dutch name "Crom Messie" or "Krom Moerasje." Sources differ as to whether this phrase meant crooked knife or crooked stream, referring to the brook that once ran east from this location.

**HUDSON RIVER PARK** The area between the Joe DiMaggio Highway and the Hudson River which is being developed as parkland from Chambers Street to 59th Street.

**IRVING PLACE** Though *The Legend of Sleepy Hollow* author and diplomat Washington Irving, 1783–1859, never lived on this short street, he had a nephew who did.

**LEXINGTON AVENUE** Named in 1836 for the Revolutionary War battle of Lexington (Massachusetts), this avenue was a later addition to the Commissioners' Plan of 1811. It was laid out in 1832 in response to the need for an additional north-south artery.

**NATHAN D. PERLMAN PLACE** For the associate of the Court of Special Sessions and former member of the House of Representatives. Perlman, 1887–1952, a Polish immigrant, was known for sponsoring legislation facilitating immigration and for various philanthropic endeavors. He was a president of the adjacent Beth Israel Hospital.

**PARK AVENUE SOUTH** What is now Park Avenue was originally laid out in the 1811 Commissioners' Plan as 4th Avenue. In 1832, the long narrow strip down the middle of the island was granted to the New York and Harlem Railroad which ran horse-drawn cars along its path starting with a run between Union Square and 23rd Street. Steam-powered locomotives were soon introduced here, but public outcry forced the line to revert to horse power in 1846. In 1860 the stretch of 4th Avenue below Murray Hill was renamed Park Avenue partly because a still-existing tunnel, at the time topped with a landscaped garden, had been cut through for the trains between 34th and 38th Streets. Below 42nd Street the avenue is designated as "South."

**POLICE OFFICER ANTHONY SANCHEZ WAY** Named in 1997 to honor a much-decorated police officer who was killed in the line of duty that year. The Police Academy is located nearby on 20th Street.

*Peter Stuyvesant*

**RUTHERFORD PLACE** For Colonel John Rutherford, one of the commissioners appointed in 1807 to lay out Manhattan Island in a grid of streets and blocks above Houston Street.

**SISTER MARY IRENE FITZGIBBON CORNER** This corner was named in 1997 for the Sisters of Charity nun whose work with poor and abandoned children of the city led to the 1864 creation of the Foundling Hospital located on this block. Fitzgibbon lived from 1823 to 1896.

**SPECIAL AGENT EVERETT E. HATCHER PLACE** Named in 1996 for the Drug Enforcement Administration agent killed in an undercover operation. The D.E.A. regional office is nearby.

**STUYVESANT SQUARE** Peter Stuyvesant, 1610–1672, was the last Dutch governor of New Netherland. His "bowerji," or farm, included this area.

**THEODORE ROOSEVELT WAY** Named in 1995 for the only native of New York City to become president. Roosevelt was born on East 20th Street in 1858, served as president of the New York City Board of Police Commissioners, and as assistant secretary of the Navy. In 1898 he led the Rough Riders in the Spanish-American War, and was elected governor of New York State. Following the assassination of William McKinley, Roosevelt, at the time vice president, assumed the presidency and was in office from 1901 to 1909. He died in 1919.

**UNION SQUARE** Before the implementation of the 1811 Commissioners' Plan to lay out Manhattan Island in a grid form, the Bowery and Broadway crossed here at an irregular angle. The new streets and avenues dictated by the grid plan produced an awkward intersection here. The solution was to leave a public plaza, today's Union Square, named for the union of these thoroughfares. The square has been a traditional rallying place for labor and political protests.

*Union Square ca. 1850*

# Kips Bay & Murray Hill

At the time the Commissioners' Plan for laying out Manhattan Island in a grid of blocks and streets was being contemplated, these areas were farms, estates, or open land belonging to the city corporation. The historic names that have survived the imposition of the numbered streets and avenues attest to landowners whose accomplishments or holdings were significant enough to remain enduringly associated with the areas. Hendrick Hendricksen Kip was a Dutch settler and the progenitor of the Kip family in New Amsterdam. His son, Jacob Hendricksen Kip, established a farm near present-day 35th Street and 2nd Avenue. Three generations of Kips succeeded Jacob in owning the property until 1851 when their mansion was demolished. Robert Murray, an 18th-century merchant, bought land for a country estate just north of Kip's property. The story goes that in 1776 British soldiers crossed the East

River from Brooklyn in preparation for taking Manhattan and cutting off the rebel forces which at the time were in lower Manhattan. Mrs. Murray, a gracious hostess, delayed the British officers in her home long enough for General Putnam's troops to speed north to join George Washington and so elude being trapped by the British. The introduction of the railroad on 4th Avenue in the 1830s accelerated residential development in the western sections of both of these neighborhoods, and by the 1850s factories and lumber yards crowded the riverfront. While the vagaries of Manhattan real estate have had their effects here, Murray Hill's quiet, residential character has been zealously and successfully guarded by its denizens, in part due to a covenant put into place by Murray's descendants which restricted the area's land use. Kips Bay's row house past remains evident, though bracketed on the east by the Kips Bay apartment complex and three medical centers, and on the west by Indian foodie heaven.

ASSER LEVY PLACE  Named for one of New Amsterdam's early Jewish settlers. Levy, a Sephardic refugee from Brazil, lobbied the anti-Semitic Peter Stuyvesant for rights for his coreligionists. It is thought that he was the first Jew to own property in New Amsterdam.

BELLEVUE PARK SOUTH  The adjacent hospital and this park take their names from an estate that stood here in the 18th century.

BROADWAY ALLEY  No reason has been found for the naming of this alley running from 26th to 27th Streets between 3rd and Lexington Avenues, though its name appears on maps as early as 1860.

ESQUINA HERMANOS AL RESCATE/BROTHERS TO THE RESCUE CORNER  The sign commemorates the members of a Miami-based anti-Castro organization whose planes were shot down by the Cuban military in 1996 while on a search-and-rescue mission over the Florida straits. The corner is diagonally across the street from the Cuban Mission to the U.N.

HERMAN MELVILLE SQUARE  Named in 1984 for the author of *Moby Dick* who lived at 104 East 26th Street from 1863 until his death in 1891. While residing in the city, Melville supported himself by working as a customs inspector on the docks named for his grandfather (see Gansevoort Street in the West Village).

JOHN McKEAN SQUARE  Named in 1993 for the real estate executive who was a respected tenant and community advocate and 20-year president of the Tudor City Association. In 1980, McKean rallied his neighbors and successfully prevented the destruction of two parks in the Tudor City apartment/hotel complex located east of 2nd Avenue between 40th and 43rd Streets.

LEXINGTON AVENUE  Named in 1836 for the Revolutionary War battle of Lexington (Massachusetts), this avenue was a later addition to the Commissioners' Plan of 1811. It was laid out in 1832 in response to the need for an additional north-south artery.

*Nelson Mandela*

MADISON AVENUE  As with Lexington Avenue, Madison was a later addition to the Commissioners' Plan. It was opened in 1836 and named for President James Madison who died that year.

MOUNT CARMEL PLACE  In 1989 Our Lady of the Scapular Church on East 28th Street petitioned for this street to be named in commemoration of the 100th anniversary of the arrival of Carmelite priests in New York City.

NELSON AND WINNIE MANDELA CORNER  Named in 1985 to honor the long-imprisoned South African leader and his then wife.

**PARK AVENUE SOUTH** What is now Park Avenue was originally laid out in the 1811 Commissioners' Plan as 4th Avenue. In 1832 the long, narrow strip down the middle of the island was granted to the New York and Harlem Railroad which ran horse-drawn cars along its path starting with a run between Union Square and 23rd Street. Steam-powered locomotives were soon introduced here, but public outcry forced the line to revert to horse power as far north as 32nd Street in 1846, and to 42nd Street in 1854. In 1860 the stretch of 4th Avenue below Murray Hill was renamed Park Avenue partly because a still-existing tunnel, at the time topped with a landscaped garden, had been cut through for the trains between 34th and 38th Streets. Below 42nd Street the avenue is designated as "South."

**PERSHING SQUARE** For John Joseph Pershing, 1860–1948, World War I commander of the American Expeditionary Forces in Europe.

**ST. VARTAN PARK** Named in 1978 for the Armenian National Cathedral located on 1st Avenue and 35th Street which faces the park.

**SAMUEL D. LEIDESDORF PLAZA** Named in 1996 for the founder of the accounting firm S. D. Leidesdorf who was noted for his philanthropic efforts in the service of medical and educational institutions. Leidesdorf's energies contributed to the development of adjacent New York University Medical Center.

**SNIFFEN COURT** Though there is some dissension as to Sniffen's identity, it is generally assumed that he was the builder/architect of this tiny group of historic buildings erected as stables in the mid-19th century.

**TRYGVE LIE PLAZA** Named for the Norwegian statesman elected in 1946 as the first secretary-general of the United Nations. Lie was reelected in 1950 and died in 1968.

**TUDOR CITY PLACE** A street in the apartment/hotel complex of the same name located east of 2nd Avenue between 40th and 43rd Streets. A self-contained Tudor-style city-within-the-city, it was completed in 1928.

**VINCENT F. ALBANO JR. PARK** Named in 1981 for the political and community leader whose efforts focused on the East Side around Tudor City.

**YITZHAK RABIN WAY** Israeli statesman Rabin held the office of Israel's prime minister from 1974 to 1977, and again from 1992 until his assassination in 1995.

*Yitzhak Rabin*

# NoMad

Edged by the Fashion District on the west and by the newish restaurant paradise on Park and Madison Avenues on the east, the neighborhood NOrth of MADison Square Park is one of those in-between areas currently experiencing a renaissance of sorts. Prized, ironically, for its lack of a cohesive identity, NoMad is drawing a residential population fond of the prices and the edgy quality of a neighborhood that may or may not become one. The southern anchor of the district is Madison Square Park, a former military parade ground which was the next stop of the entertainment center that decamped from Union Square at the end of the 19th century. Madison Square Garden didn't get its name for nothing, there having been two incarnations of it—in 1879 and 1890—on 26th Street and Madison Avenue. The city's best hotels and restaurants clustered here and the park borders boasted stately residences whose moment in the sun, though bright, was brief, as trade moved in and took over. Subsequent

eras brought hulking office structures to the environs of the

park, most notably those housing insurance giants and the

wholesale toy, Christmas ornament, and tabletop markets.

Advertising firms hold fast to their historic addresses on

Madison Avenue, and Silicon Alley, the new kid in town,

nudges from the south and west. Grand Central Terminal and

the New York Public Library, both paragons of the late 19th-

century desire to establish municipal monuments worthy of

a great city, adorn the northern end of NoMad. What is

undoubtedly the city's most visible landmark punctuates the

skyline south of these two venerable edifices. The Empire State

Building, completed at the height of the Depression, towers

over an  array of small businesses and large, from the flower

and ribbon markets to the shopping meccas of Macy's, Lord

and Taylor, and the dear-departed B. Altman & Co.

**AVENUE OF THE AMERICAS** In 1945, Mayor Fiorello La Guardia added this designation to the name of 6th Avenue to honor the ideals shared by this country and our sister pan-American nations.

**BROADWAY** Originally an Indian trail that ran north from the southern tip of Manhattan, Broadway now extends from the Battery into the Bronx. The street's name derives from its unusual width.

**BRYANT PARK** Named in 1884 for William Cullen Bryant, editor of the *New York Evening Post* from 1829 until his death in 1878. Bryant was instrumental in the creation of such civic landmarks as Central Park and the Metropolitan Museum of Art. His pen and voice were influential in many arenas, particularly as they expressed his stance against slavery.

*William Cullen Bryant*

**GOLDA MEIR SQUARE** Meir was prime minister of Israel from 1969 to 1974 and died in 1987. This section of Broadway was given her name in 1979.

**GREELEY SQUARE** Horace Greeley, 1811–1872, founded the *New York Tribune* in 1841, and was an outspoken political leader. Commonly credited with the phrase "Go West, young man," Greeley actually adopted it from an Indiana journalist.

**HERALD SQUARE** Named for the *New York Herald* whose offices were nearby on 35th Street for 40 years starting in 1893. The newspaper was edited by James Gordon Bennett, Sr. from 1835 to 1867, and until 1918 by his son, James Gordon Bennett, Jr.

*Horace Greeley*

**HERMAN MELVILLE SQUARE** Named in 1984 for the author of *Moby Dick* who lived at 104 East 26th Street from 1863 until his death in 1891. While residing in the city, Melville supported himself by working as a customs inspector on the docks named for his grandfather (see Gansevoort Street in the West Village).

**KOREA WAY** The area's vibrant Korean business presence emerged in the 1970s and was recognized in 1995 with the naming of this block of Broadway.

**MADISON AVENUE** This avenue was a later addition to the 1811 Commissioners' Plan. It was opened in 1836 and named for President James Madison who died that year.

NoMad

**MADISON SQUARE PARK** A potter's field at the end of the 18th century, and in subsequent years an army arsenal and military parade ground, the square was named for President James Madison in 1814. Opened to the public in 1847, the park had the distinction of hosting the right, torch-clutching hand of the Statue of Liberty prior to its being exhibited at the Philadelphia Centennial Exposition in 1876. The hand joined the rest of Miss Liberty when the statue was erected on Liberty Island in 1886. The first and second Madison Square Gardens were situated at 26th Street and Madison Avenue from 1879 to 1924.

*The Statue of Liberty's hand was displayed in Madison Square Park.*

**NIKOLA TESLA CORNER** Designated in 1992 for the Croatian immigrant and electrical engineer who was awarded the Nobel Prize in 1912 for his invention of the induction motor and other innovations in the field of electricity. Tesla declined the prize, attesting that it was honor enough to have had his inventions featured in countless scientific publications.

**NORMAN VINCENT PEALE WAY** Named in 1998 for the pastor of Marble Collegiate Church. Peale, who died in 1993, hosted a radio program which was heard for 54 years, started *Guideposts*, a religious magazine, and in 1952 published the book *The Power of Positive Thinking*.

**NYC 2000 WAY** Broadway between 42nd and 47th Streets was so dubbed in conjunction with the millennium celebrations that took place in Times Square.

**PARK AVENUE SOUTH** What is now Park Avenue was originally laid out in the 1811 Commissioners' Plan as 4th Avenue. In 1832, the long, narrow strip down the middle of the island was granted to the New York and Harlem Railroad which ran horse-drawn cars along its path starting with a run between Union Square and 23rd Street. Steam-powered locomotives were soon introduced here, but public outcry forced the line to revert to horse power as far north as 32nd Street in 1846, and to 42nd Street in 1854. In 1860 the stretch of 4th Avenue below Murray Hill was renamed Park Avenue partly because a still-existing tunnel, at the time topped with a landscaped garden, had been cut through for the trains between 34th and 38th Streets. Below 42nd Street the avenue is designated as "South."

**SHOLOM ALEICHEM PLACE** This corner was named in 1996 for the beloved Yiddish author of the *Tevye Stories* which were the basis for the Broadway show *Fiddler on the Roof*. An immigrant from the Ukraine, the author was born in 1859 and died in 1916 in the Bronx.

**WORTH SQUARE** For Major General William Jennings Worth, 1794–1849, second in command to Zachary Taylor in the Mexican War. Worth is said to have been the first to plant the American flag at the Rio Grande. He died in this conflict and is buried under the monument at this location. Worth's valor inspired the name of Fort Worth, Texas.

# Lower West Side & Fashion Center

To a large extent, the arrival of the Hudson River Railroad in the 1840s dictated the development of the west side of the city. Rolling hills and country estates were plowed under as the unbeatable team of water transportation, rail links, and industry joined forces. As had happened just to the south, this area became a chugging engine of iron foundries, coal sheds, lumber and stone yards, and abattoirs—along with rail yards and other facilities supporting the iron horse. Tenements housing workers in these industries swarmed to the east. Two colorful names are associated with the district: Hell's Kitchen refers to a gang which terrorized the neighborhood and regularly robbed the trains in the 30th Street rail yards in the 1880s and 1890s; the Tenderloin, also part of this section, owes its name to a police captain's delight at being stationed on this beat where his takings on the side would allow him to exchange chuck steak for the finer cut. By the 1960s the tenements had been razed to make way for large housing projects which now dot the area. The rail yards are still in the West 30s but the factories have given way to UPS and FedEx terminals, Port Authority Bus Station, the Central Post Office, and the Jacob Javits Convention Center. New York City's identity as the fashion capital of at least this country is rendered visible on 7th Avenue and the side streets running through it in the West 30s. Runners pushing racks of clothes dodge zanily through a welter of traffic, and runway models stride to showrooms in the buildings above. Penn Station and Madison Square Garden, Siamese twins of sport and transport, create their own traffic frenzies. Farther south in the West 20s, warehouse behemoths which had seen better days are being given new life as Silicon Alley whiz kids flock to their wide-open spaces. With all these e-brains around, could a restaurant scene be far behind?

**AVENUE OF THE AMERICAS** In 1945, Mayor Fiorello La Guardia added this designation to the name of 6th Avenue to honor the ideals shared by this country and our sister pan-American nations.

**BROADWAY** Originally an Indian trail that ran north from the southern tip of Manhattan, Broadway now extends from the Battery into the Bronx. The street's name derives from its unusual width.

**CARDINAL STEPINAC PLACE** Stepinac, who died in 1960, was a Croatian cleric brought to trial by the Tito regime on charges of collaboration with the Nazis. He was sentenced to serve 16 years but was released after five as the Yugoslav government feared he would be hailed as a martyr. The Croatian Church of St. Cyril & Methodius is on this block in the heart of the city's Croatian community which congregated here at the end of the 19th century.

**CHELSEA PARK** The estate that once graced this part of Manhattan up to about 28th Street gave the area just to the south its name. The mid-18th-century owner, Captain Thomas Clarke, christened it to recall the grounds of London's Royal Hospital at Chelsea. Clarke was the grandfather of Clement Clarke Moore, author of *'Twas the Night Before Christmas*.

**DYER STREET** This traffic funnel to the Lincoln Tunnel was named for Major General George Rathbone Dyer, 1869–1934. As chairman of the New York State Bridge and Tunnel Commission, and later of the Port of New York Authority, Dyer was a key figure in the creation of the Holland and Lincoln Tunnels.

*Clement Clarke Moore*

**FASHION AVENUE** This section of 7th Avenue acknowledges New York City's stature as fashion capital of the world.

**HUDSON GUILD PLACE** Founded in 1895 by John Lovejoy Elliott, the Hudson Guild was a settlement house providing services to immigrants in Chelsea. It now hosts community theater productions and after-school programs for children. This part of 26th Street was named in 1995 in celebration of the organization's centennial.

**HUDSON RIVER PARK** The area between the Joe DiMaggio Highway and the Hudson River which is being developed as parkland from Chambers Street to 59th Street.

**JOE LOUIS PLAZA** Joe Louis, 1914–1981, held boxing's heavyweight championship for 12 years, from 1937 to 1949, a record surpassing that of any other fighter. This spot adjoining Madison Square Garden was named in 1984 as a tribute to Louis's achievement.

**MILLENNIUM WAY** As part of the millennium celebration in Times Square, these blocks of 7th Avenue were given an honorary title.

**NEW 42ND STREET** The new moniker of West 42nd Street between 7th and 8th Avenues reflects the in-progress sanitizing of this erstwhile hub of New York's honky-tonk adult entertainment district.

*Joe Louis*

# Midtown

*8th Avenue*

59th Street

*Lexington Avenue*

*12th Avenue*

Clinton

## Central Midtown
*and*
## Entertainment
## District

## East
## Midtown

*FDR Drive*

42nd Street

# East Midtown

East Midtown's history echoes that of other riverside locations of the city in their evolution from open country to estates and farms, later to factories and tenements, followed by mixed commercial and residential uses. A distinguishing feature of this neighborhood is the survival of tiny, upscale, river-view residential enclaves redolent of an earlier era. Beekman and Sutton Places are indicated by street signs and are discussed below. Turtle Bay, the oldest place name of the three, has no such visible labels and earned its name in one of two ways. Some believe it arose from the turtle-filled cove that existed there into the 19th century; others contend that it comes from the cove's being shaped like a knife blade – "deutal" in Dutch. Turtle Bay's appealing row houses are greatly prized and have attracted residents from the theater and literary worlds. The 1952 completion of the United Nations rid the area of its remaining unsightly industrial occu-

Midtown

pants, among them slaughterhouses and breweries, and set off

a frenzy of renaming streets in honor of diplomatic figures.

Several luxury apartment buildings house locals as well as the

myriad of United Nations delegates and employees. All of these

will soon be dwarfed by the controversial Trump World Tower

shooting skyward on 1st Avenue and 47th Street. West from

here to Lexington Avenue a host of apartment and office build-

ings of various shapes, sizes, and vintages provides living and

working space for all manner of local businesses and residents.

**ABP Fulton J. Sheen Place** Named in 1980 for Archbishop Sheen, 1895–1979, whose radio and television shows brought him national recognition.

**Allard K. Lowenstein Place** Lowenstein, 1929–1980, was an attorney and congressman who advocated for civil rights and against the Vietnam War in the 1960s. He was shot and killed in his office by a former co-worker in 1980.

**Beekman Place** The mansion of the Beekman family was situated here from 1765 to 1874. The British, who held the city during the Revolution, convicted Nathan Hale of spying and executed him on the Beekman property in 1776.

*The Beekman family's mansion, 1861.*

East Midtown

**DAG HAMMARSKJOLD PLAZA**  Swedish diplomat Hammarskjold, 1905–1961, served as secretary-general of the United Nations from 1953 until his death in an airplane crash in Africa. Hammarskjold was posthumously awarded the Nobel Peace Prize for his work to bring peace to the Congo. This plaza was named for him in 1961.

*Douglas MacArthur*

**GENERAL DOUGLAS MACARTHUR PLAZA & MACARTHUR PARK**  MacArthur's famous promise "I shall return," proclaimed after he left the Philippines in 1942, was fulfilled two years later. A veteran of World War I, MacArthur was appointed in 1941 by President Franklin Delano Roosevelt to be commander of the Army in the Far East, and later commander of the Allied forces in the Southwest Pacific. At the conclusion of the war, MacArthur oversaw the Allied occupation of Japan. He served with distinction in the Korean War as well, though disagreements with President Truman led to removal of his command. MacArthur and his father, a hero of the Civil War, are the only father and son ever to have received the Medal of Honor. MacArthur died in 1964.

**ISRAEL BONDS WAY**  This corner of East 52nd Street and Lexington Avenue recognizes the organization whose offices moved to this location in 1994. Since its inception in 1951, State of Israel Bonds has been a vehicle for investors worldwide to contribute to the development of Israel.

**KATHARINE HEPBURN GARDEN**  The legendary American actress first moved to the Turtle Bay neighborhood in 1932. The garden in Dag Hammarskjold Plaza, named for her in 1997, commemorates Hepburn's lifelong delight in gardening as well as her support of the Turtle Bay Association in its efforts to preserve the charm of this tiny enclave.

**KUDIRAT ABIOLA CORNER**  Installed in 1997, this sign commemorates the murdered wife of Nigerian Chief Moshood Abiola. Though Chief Abiola was elected president of Nigeria in 1993, he was jailed when the election was annulled by the military regime of General Ibrahim Babangida. Kudirat continued to agitate for her husband's release and for democracy, but was murdered in 1996. Chief Abiola died in prison in 1999.

**LEXINGTON AVENUE**  Named in 1836 for the Revolutionary War battle of Lexington (Massachusetts), this avenue was a later addition to the Commissioners' Plan of 1811. It was laid out in 1832 in response to the need for an additional north-south artery.

**MITCHELL PLACE**  This short portion of 49th Street east of 1st Avenue was named in 1871 for William Mitchell, 1801–1886, an esteemed lawyer, one-time vice president of the New York Bar Association, justice of the State Supreme Court, and judge of the Court of Appeals. Mitchell was a descendant of Peter Anderson to whom the Dutch West India Company granted land in Turtle Bay in 1645.

**PETER DETMOLD PARK** Named in 1972 for the real estate executive who was active in the affairs of the Turtle Bay neighborhood and served as president of the tenants' association. His stabbing death that year occasioned the dedication of this park.

**RALPH J. BUNCHE PARK** Consistent with its location near the United Nations, this park name honors a diplomat. Ralph Bunche, 1904–1971, was awarded the Nobel Peace Prize in 1950 for his efforts in crafting the Arab-Israeli agreement of 1948–1949. Bunche was under-secretary of the U.N. from 1955 until his death in 1971.

**RAOUL WALLENBERG WALK** At the behest of the Raoul Wallenberg Committee of the United States, 1st Avenue across from the U.N. was named in 1985 for the heroic Swedish diplomat who engineered the rescue of thousands of Hungarian Jews during World War II. Wallenberg was arrested by Soviet authorities in 1945 and disappeared into the Soviet prison system. His fate is unknown.

*Raoul Wallenberg*

**RIVERVIEW TERRACE** A terrace from which to view the river at the east end of Sutton Square.

**SHARANSKY STEPS** Anatoly Shcharansky, a Russian, was arrested in Moscow in 1977 on suspicion of being a spy for the C.I.A. He was released nine years later in a spy-swapping deal and emigrated to Israel. Having changed his name to Natan Sharansky, he is, as of this writing, interior minister of Israel.

**SUTTON PLACE, SUTTON PLACE PARK & SUTTON SQUARE** One of Manhattan's most prestigious addresses, this short "riv vu" extension of York Avenue was developed as blocks of row houses by Effingham B. Sutton who bought the land in 1875. At the time, the banks of the East River were pocked with factories and tenements. In the 1920s, members of the Vanderbilt and Morgan haut monde discovered and recovered Effingham's row houses, and Sutton Place's noble lineage was launched.

**UNITED NATIONS PLAZA** The stretch of 1st Avenue from 43rd to 49th Streets pays tribute to the United Nations which opened in 1952.

**YITZHAK RABIN WAY** Israeli statesman Rabin held the office of Israel's prime minister from 1974 to 1977, and again from 1992 until his assassination in 1995.

East Midtown

# Central Midtown & Entertainment District

Central Midtown is Manhattan's big-business and entertainment hub. The monumental office towers on Park, Madison, 5th, and 6th Avenues pulse with the executives and worker bees of the giants of broadcasting, publishing, the law, and countless other fields. All this industry is offset and enriched by such icons of earlier eras as St. Patrick's Cathedral, Rockefeller Center, and Radio City Music Hall. Fifth Avenue, once studded with mansions of the very very very rich, is now totally devoted to retail and business interests, with a few clubs, churches, and hotels thrown in. Nonetheless, despite its decline from fashionable shopping destination to electronic gadgetville, the avenue is holding its own with bastions like Saks Fifth Avenue, Bergdorf Goodman, and Tiffany's still packing them in. Spreading out from Times Square in the southwest corner of

Central Midtown is the Entertainment District, a mantle inherited from Madison Square to the south when the Metropolitan Opera House repositioned itself at Broadway and 39th Street in 1883. The development of mass transportation crisscrossing Times Square sealed its role as the crossroads of the city and the district's glitzy/sleazy reputation that was so well deserved and so well loved emerged early on. Everything from girlie shows to freak shows, along with high-end "legitimate" venues and restaurants, made this hurly-burly nexus a symbol of the high-wire excitement of New York. Now in the midst of a "redevelopment," 42nd Street and Times Square are being rendered squeaky clean by the likes of Disney, Loew's, and Madame Tussaud's. Despite, or perhaps because of, the new, oh-so-wholesome image, the legitimate theater thrives, and, along with television studios, movie theaters, Radio City Music Hall, and top-notch restaurants, the white way remains great.

**ACTORS' SQUARE** It should come as no surprise that a sign honoring actors exists in Times Square (in Duffy Square to be precise). As of this writing, however, the vitals on this sign (who put it up, when, and why) remain a mystery.

**ADOLPH S. OCHS STREET** Named in 1996 for the longtime publisher of the *New York Times*. Ochs, 1858–1935, purchased the paper in 1896, saving it from bankruptcy. He developed the *Times* into the purveyor of "All the News That's Fit to Print," and passed its ownership to succeeding generations of his family.

**AVENUE OF THE AMERICAS** In 1945, Mayor Fiorello La Guardia added this designation to the name of 6th Avenue to honor the ideals shared by this country and our sister pan-American nations.

*Adolph S. Ochs*

**BIG APPLE CORNER** For those readers who have always wondered why the city came to be known as the Big Apple, the City Council proceedings of 1997 offer the following explanations. John J. Fitzgerald, a 1920s journalist specializing in horse racing, had apparently heard African-American stable hands in New Orleans use the term to refer to New York City as having the top-rated racecourses. Fitzgerald, who lived at 54th Street and Broadway, adopted the name for his column *Around the Big Apple*. Another possible origin is the jazz world where musicians called New York City the Big Apple as an allusion to its being the jazz capital of the world.

**BROADWAY** Originally an Indian trail that ran north from the southern tip of Manhattan, Broadway now extends from the Battery into the Bronx. The street's name derives from its unusual width.

**COUSIN BRUCIE WAY** A street sign near the headquarters of WCBS-FM was installed at the request of Hosteling International New York to recognize the efforts of this popular and ageless radio personality in his role as spokesperson for Bike New York, the yearly 42-mile bike ride through the five boroughs of the city. The sign above this one pays tribute to the radio station for sponsoring the event. The 23rd ride took place in 2000.

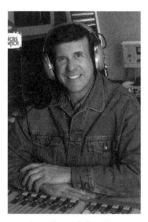

**DEPEW PLACE** Running along the east side of Grand Central Terminal, this passage is currently more an alley than a place. Its namesake is Chauncey M. Depew, 1834–1928, a lawyer, New York secretary of state, president of New York Central Railroad, and U.S. senator. Depew was noted for his talent as a public speaker, and volumes of his speeches were published.

*Cousin Brucie*

**DIAMOND & JEWELRY WAY** 47th Street between 5th and 6th Avenues is just what the name indicates—the center of the city's wholesale and retail diamond and jewelry market. The street was given this designation in 1982.

**DORIS C. FREEDMAN PLAZA** Freedman, 1928–1981, was the daughter of architect and builder Irwin Chanin (as in the Chanin Building on East 42nd Street). In her capacity as the first director of the New York City Department of Cultural Affairs from 1967 to 1970, Freedman promoted the use of art in public spaces around the city.

**DUFFY SQUARE** Obscured by the TKTS tent is a statue of Father Francis P. Duffy, chaplain of the Fighting 69th, an all-Irish division of the 165th Infantry. While the unit's proud history goes back to the Civil War, Duffy served with them in the trenches of World War I and received the Distinguished Service Cross for his valor. His home parish was on West 42nd Street where he ministered to the troopers of the theater world until his death in 1932.

**GEORGE ABBOTT WAY** Immortalized here is the writer, director, and producer of such Broadway smash hits as *The Pajama Game*, *Damn Yankees*, and *A Funny Thing Happened on the Way to the Forum*. Abbott died in 1995 at the age of 107, shortly after supervising the revival of *Damn Yankees*.

**GOOD MORNING AMERICA WAY** This popular morning television show is taped at the ABC studios on the corner.

**GRAND ARMY PLAZA** This graceful plaza in front of the Plaza Hotel extends north and south of 59th Street at 5th Avenue. The northern portion sports a dazzling equestrian statue of Civil War General William Tecumseh Sherman which was installed in 1903, and the south is centered on the Pulitzer Memorial "Fountain of Youth." Though the open space had been created as part of the design of Central Park, the whole ensemble was not completed until 1912. The name, conferred in 1923, refers to the Grand Army of the Republic, a veterans' organization whose mission was to honor the soldiers who fought for the Union during the Civil War.

**JACK DEMPSEY CORNER** Dempsey, 1895–1983, was a popular heavyweight champion celebrated for his record number of first-round knockouts and his 1927 defeat by Gene Tunney. After retiring, Dempsey opened a restaurant on this corner where he could often be seen sitting at a table by the window. The corner was named in 1984.

**LEON DAVIS STREET** Located near the headquarters of Local 1199 of the drug, hospital, and health-care employees, this block of West 43rd Street is named for the union's president who died in 1992 after 50 years of service.

*Jack Dempsey*

**LEXINGTON AVENUE** Named in 1836 for the Revolutionary War battle of Lexington (Massachusetts), this avenue was a later addition to the Commissioners' Plan of 1811. It was laid out in 1832 in response to the need for an additional north-south artery.

**LIGHTHOUSE WAY** Lighthouse International, the non-profit organization dedicated to addressing the needs of the visually challenged, has occupied this site on 59th Street between Park and Lexington Avenues since 1913. The street sign went up in 1994 to mark the completion of the building's renovation.

**LITTLE BRAZIL STREET** West 46th Street between 5th Avenue and Broadway is known as one of the centers of Brazilian life in the city. The fact that most businesses on this street are owned by Brazilians was recognized by the 1996 street naming.

**MADISON AVENUE** This avenue was a later addition to the Commissioners' Plan of 1811. It was opened in 1836 and named for President James Madison who died that year.

**MILLENNIUM WAY** As part of the millennium celebration in Times Square, these blocks of 7th Avenue were given an honorary title.

**NEW 42ND STREET** The new moniker of West 42nd Street between 7th and 8th Avenues reflects the in-progress sanitizing of this erstwhile hub of New York's honky-tonk adult entertainment district.

**NYC 2000 WAY** Broadway between 42nd and 47th Streets was so dubbed in conjunction with the millennium celebrations that took place in Times Square.

**PARK AVENUE** What is now Park Avenue was originally laid out in the 1811 Commissioners' Plan as 4th Avenue. In 1832, the long, narrow strip down the middle of the island was granted to the New York and Harlem Railroad which ran horse-drawn cars along its path starting with a run between Union Square and 23rd Street. By 1834, the service operated from Prince Street to the Upper East Side. Though given its present name in 1888, it was the 1903 conversion from steam to electric train power and the 1913 completion of the present Grand Central Terminal that paved the way for Park Avenue's classy future. The previously open rail yards and tracks north of the terminal were covered over by the 1920s and the avenue's wide, landscaped center medians gave credibility to its name. The rest is social registry and, later, corporate history.

**RESTAURANT ROW** West 46th Street between 8th and 9th Avenues has earned the title due to its high concentration of theater district restaurants.

**ROCKEFELLER PLAZA** A short north-south roadway that bisects the Rockefeller Center complex, the original buildings of which were erected from 1932 to 1940, and are considered icons of the Art Deco style. As mastermind and master of money, John D. Rockefeller, Jr. is the complex's namesake.

**RODGERS & HAMMERSTEIN ROW** This corner of the theater district was named on the 50th anniversary of the composer and lyricist partnership of Richard Rodgers, 1902–1979, and Oscar Hammerstein II, 1895–1960. Together, these two legends of the American musical theater created such beloved Broadway shows as *Oklahoma!* (1943), *Carousel* (1945), *South Pacific* (1949), *The King and I* (1951), and *The Sound of Music* (1959). Eight of their nine Broadway musicals premiered in theaters here on West 44th Street.

**SEÑOR WENCES WAY** Those old enough to have been brought up on the *Ed Sullivan Show* will recall with fondness the characters created from the hand of ex-bullfighter/ventriloquist Wenceslao Moreno, aka Señor Wences. Wences/Moreno died in 1999 at the age of 103, prompting the street-sign tribute on this corner near the Ed Sullivan Theater.

**SHUBERT ALLEY** Bisecting the block from West 44th to West 45th Streets between Broadway and 7th Avenue is a short passage identified by a plaque on the east side of the Shubert Theater which commemorates "all those who glorify the theater." The Shubert family developed its theater syndicate in the 19th century, and remains a major force in the industry.

**SWING STREET** In the 1930s and 1940s, 52nd Street was the place to go for jazz and dancing.

**TIMES SQUARE** Until the early 20th century, this crossroads was known as Longacre Square and was the center of the city's carriage supply industry. The name was adopted from a district in London where similar businesses congregated. The 1904 erection of *The New York Times* building on 43rd Street prompted the reinvention of the area and the name change.

*Cornelius Vanderbilt*

**VANDERBILT AVENUE** Commodore Cornelius Vanderbilt, 1794–1877, merged two previously existing railroads—the New York and Harlem line, and the New York and Hudson River line—to form the New York Central and Hudson River Railroad. The first Grand Central Terminal located at 42nd Street and 4th Avenue was constructed at Vanderbilt's behest in 1871. The present structure, completed in 1913, replaced the original. This north-south thoroughfare on the west side of the terminal, declared a public street in 1869, reminds us of the transportation genius who made it all happen.

Central Midtown & Entertainment District

**WCBS-FM WAY/PROUD SPONSOR OF BIKE NEW YORK** A street sign near the headquarters of the radio station was installed at the request of Hosteling International New York to thank WCBS-FM for sponsoring Bike New York, their yearly 42-mile bike ride through the five boroughs of the city. The sign just below this one pays tribute to radio personality Cousin Brucie for his efforts as spokesperson of the event. The 23rd annual ride took place in 2000.

**W. C. HANDY'S PLACE** Composer, musician, and blues legend Handy, 1873–1958, was responsible for such classics as *Memphis Blues* and *St. Louis Blues*. The placement of this sign on West 52nd Street is a nod to the street's history as a popular music and dance club venue.

# Clinton
Crossing 8th Avenue from the east in the 50s a subtle change of atmosphere becomes apparent. The flashy lights and sights of Times Square and Broadway give way to residential blocks of short and tall buildings interspersed with neighborhood stores and corner restaurants. On the northern end, Roosevelt Hospital and John Jay College of Criminal Justice, along with Columbus Circle, put a full stop to the section and provide a fitting transition to the more urbane region just uptown. Like its fellow riverside stretches to the south, Clinton has left behind its past as a 19th-century industrial blot, shedding the usual welter of abattoirs, freight yards, piers, curled hair factories, and coal yards. The masses of immigrant labor that swelled local tenements fueled the area's multinational color as well as its flare-ups of ethnic conflict which have long since been resolved as assimilation spurs coalescence. Prior to 1959, Clinton was called Hell's Kitchen

and was the northern extension of that district discussed above in the Lower West Side. Renaming the neighborhood in an effort to spiff up its reputation, residents looked to an early statesman whose name already adorned a local park. De Witt Clinton, 1769–1828, was several-time mayor of the city (terms at the time were for one year), governor of the state, and the force behind the construction of the Erie Canal. Clinton retains much of its socioeconomic diversity and neighborhood flavor, having been passed over by the rampant gentrification evident elsewhere in the city.

AMSTERDAM AVENUE What is now Amsterdam Avenue was laid out in the 1811 Commissioners' Plan as 10th Avenue and opened from 59th Street to Fort George Avenue in 1816. The name was changed in 1890 in a bid on the part of Upper West Side landowners to confer a measure of old-world cachet to their real estate investments in an area that had yet to catch on. The new avenue name supported the speculators' claim that this section would become "the New City" and a "new, New Amsterdam."

COLUMBUS AVENUE & CIRCLE As with Amsterdam Avenue above, what was originally labeled 9th Avenue on the Commissioners' Plan was changed to the more evocative Columbus Avenue in 1890. In the same year, Congress passed an act declaring that the 400th anniversary of Columbus's discovery of America would be celebrated in 1892 with an international exhibit in Chicago. The Circle was named when it was chosen as the site for a memorial to Columbus donated by the Italian population of the city. The statue of Columbus atop a column was designed by Gaetano Russo and installed in 1894.

**DE WITT CLINTON PARK** Opened in 1904, the park was named for mayor and governor De Witt Clinton, 1769–1828, who was largely responsible for the creation of the Erie Canal. The canal, inaugurated in 1825, connected the Hudson River to the Great Lakes, making New York City the most important center of trade in the country.

**HELL'S KITCHEN PARK** Lest it be forgot—the old epithet for Clinton is memorialized in this park. The name was adopted from that of a gang of hoodlums who terrorized this area in the latter part of the 19th century.

**HUDSON RIVER PARK** The area between the Joe DiMaggio Highway and the Hudson River which is being developed as parkland from Chambers Street to 59th Street.

**JOE HORVATH STREET** Joe Horvath, 1945–1995, is remembered here for his work with the youth of Hell's Kitchen. Through the Police Athletic League, he promoted sports and other recreational programs for neighborhood kids.

*De Witt Clinton*

**JOHN JAY SQUARE** Named in recognition of adjacent John Jay College of Criminal Justice and its 1980s renovation of the venerable De Witt Clinton/Haaren High School Building for use as its new base of operations. The school is named for statesman and jurist John Jay, 1745–1829.

**RESTAURANT ROW** West 46th Street between 8th and 9th Avenues has earned the title due to its high concentration of theater district restaurants.

**RUNYON'S WAY** In connection with the 1992 revival of the hit musical *Guys and Dolls* in a theater on this block, the street was named for the play's author, Damon Runyon, 1880–1946.

*Damon Runyon*

**WEST END AVENUE** Though one source asserts that the avenue took its name from the fact that the western end of the British fortifications lay along this line during the Revolution, a more likely explanation is related to the origin of Amsterdam and Columbus Avenues above. The street was laid out in the Commissioners' 1811 Plan as 11th Avenue, but the name was changed to West End Avenue in 1880 at a time when West Side landowners were anxious to attract buyers to their neighborhood. A contemporary real estate publication noted that "it was the west end of all great cities which contained the finest residences and became the fashionable centre." The blocks between 59th and 110th Streets west of Central Park were called the West End during this era, and it followed naturally that the avenue's new name should capitalize on its surroundings' much-anticipated glory.

Clinton

# East Side

141st Street

5th Avenue

Harlem River Drive

## East/Spanish Harlem

FDR Drive

98th Street

Madison Avenue

96th Street

## Upper East Side

5th Avenue

FDR Drive

59th Street

# Upper East Side

Despite its somewhat checkered past, the Upper East Side has been synonymous with "Gold Coast" since the railroad tracks running along and then under Park Avenue were covered up and planted over, and since Central Park morphed from a sinkhole of shanties, swamps, and sties to a pastoral swath originally dubbed "Greensward." In the 18th century, when the city was concentrated on the southern tip of Manhattan, the upper regions of the island were remote country, reached on the east side via the Boston Post Road which ran approximately where 2nd Avenue is today. Country estates graced the hills overlooking the East River, providing a retreat for the fortunate few from the crowding and occasional outbreak of disease that plagued the populace downtown. By the 1830s the landscape around the villages of Harlem and Yorkville was dotted with shantytowns, stock pens, garbage heaps, quarries, and farms.

Though the Commissioners' Plan was nominally put into effect in 1811, streets uptown were laid out but not developed until public transportation made the area accessible. When the railroad and trolleys began their penetration of the area—a process culminating with the construction of the 3rd Avenue elevated line in the 1870s—the real estate race took off in earnest. Block after block of brownstone row houses sprouted on the side streets between 3rd and Madison Avenues for middle-class families whose breadwinners could now easily commute to work downtown. A different story evolved east of 3rd Avenue where tenements were built to house immigrants working in the cigar factories, breweries, and other light industries that sprang up along the river, wiping out what had been country not long before. The encroaching city engulfed the village of Yorkville where a mostly German population clustered and remained until recent years. Wealthy pioneers venturing this far uptown did so cautiously and in some cases in the wake of their churches which bravely took the leap first.

Barons of the new industrial order caused palatial mansions to

be assembled on 5th and Madison Avenues, literally casting in

stone the toney future of the Upper East Side. Some of the

neighborhood names within the district reflect the hilly topog-

raphy that made it desirable to those of means. Lenox Hill

takes its name from Robert Lenox whose farm occupied 30

acres from 68th to 70th Streets west of Park Avenue in the late

18th and early 19th centuries. Andrew Carnegie may have

failed in his mission to build the "most modest, plainest" house

in the city at 91st Street and 5th Avenue, but he did succeed in

leaving his name on the hill it occupies.

**BOBBY WAGNER WALK** In the East 90s a section of the FDR Drive esplanade is a memorial to Robert Wagner III, 1944–1993, son of three-time mayor Robert F. Wagner, Jr., and
grandson of Robert F. Wagner, Sr., state and U.S. senator and justice of the New York State
Supreme Court. The younger Wagner served the city in several capacities, among them as a
member of the City Council, chairman of the City Planning Commission, and president of
the Board of Education.

**CARL SCHURZ PARK**  The park, originally opened in 1876, is named for a German-born journalist and editor, soldier, and statesman. Schurz, 1829–1906, immigrated to Wisconsin and made a name for himself speaking out against slavery. He fought in the Civil War, served as a senator from Missouri, and was appointed secretary of the interior under President Rutherford B. Hayes. Moving to New York, he became editor of the *Evening Post* and then an editorial writer for *Harper's Weekly*. Schurz lived for a time on East 91st Street.

**CHEROKEE PLACE**  The short street on the west side of John Jay Park between 77th and 78th Streets was named for the Cherokee Club, a Democratic clubhouse, which stood at 334 East 79th Street in the 1880s. The name of the clubhouse is in keeping with the Indian motif adopted by Tammany.

**EAST END AVENUE**  Laid out and named in 1876 as an extension of Avenue B, the name was changed in 1890, probably in an attempt by landowners (like those on the West Side) to confer a classier address on the neighborhood.

**FRED LEBOW PLACE**  Named for the garment industry executive whose interest in long-distance running led him to organize the New York City Marathon in 1970. The New York Road Runners Club is on this block. Lebow died in 1994.

**GEORGE & ANNETTE MURPHY SQUARE**  Longtime Upper East Side residents, the Murphys were instrumental in developing the Asphalt Green recreational complex housed in the former Municipal Asphalt Plant. The square was named in 1987.

**GRACIE SQUARE**  Archibald Gracie, 1755–1829, a successful merchant from Scotland, acquired a country estate overlooking the East River here in the early years of the 19th century. The mansion he built has been the official New York City mayor's residence since 1942.

**GRAND ARMY PLAZA**  This graceful plaza in front of the Plaza Hotel extends north and south of 59th Street at 5th Avenue. The northern portion sports a dazzling equestrian statue of General William Tecumseh Sherman installed in 1903, and the south is centered on the Pulitzer Memorial "Fountain of Youth." Though the open space had been created as part of the design of Central Park, the whole ensemble was not completed until 1912. The name, conferred in 1923, refers to the Grand Army of the Republic, a veterans' organization whose mission was to honor the soldiers who fought for the Union during the Civil War.

**HENDERSON PLACE**  This gemlike grouping of rowhouses tucked just off East 86th Street and East End Avenue was developed between 1881 and 1882 by merchant John C. Henderson. Henderson used the houses as rental properties and gave the cul-de-sac his name.

**JAMES CAGNEY PLACE**  This block of East 91st Street was named for the tough-guy actor in 1989. Born on the Lower East Side in 1899, Cagney was brought up in Yorkville, living at various times on East 79th and East 96th Streets. For extra money, the young Cagney worked several jobs, among them stacking books at the Lenox Hill Settlement House (see below). Cagney's funeral was held in St. Francis de Sales Roman Catholic Church on East 96th Street where he had been confirmed and served as an altar boy.

**JOHN JAY PARK** The city acquired the land for the park in 1902 and named it for the statesman and jurist who died in 1829. In 1789 Jay was appointed by George Washington to be the first chief justice of the United States. He negotiated the Jay Treaty which ended the Revolution, and served two terms as governor of New York State.

*John Jay*

**LENOX HILL NEIGHBORHOOD HOUSE WAY** In 1994, on the occasion of the settlement house's centennial, this portion of East 70th Street was given the organization's name. The Neighborhood House continues to provide social services for local residents and it retains the name of Robert Lenox whose farm occupied 30 acres west of this location in the late 18th and early 19th century.

**LEXINGTON AVENUE** Named in 1836 for the Revolutionary War battle of Lexington (Massachusetts), this avenue was a later addition to the Commissioners' Plan of 1811. It was laid out in 1832 in response to the need for an additional north-south artery.

**LIGHTHOUSE WAY** Lighthouse International, the non-profit organization dedicated to addressing the needs of the visually challenged, has occupied this site on 59th Street between Park and Lexington Avenues since 1913. The street sign went up in 1994 to mark the completion of the building's renovation.

**MADISON AVENUE** Like Lexington Avenue, this thoroughfare was a later addition to the Commissioners' Plan of 1811. It was opened in 1836 and named for President James Madison who died that year.

**MUSEUM MILE** Fifth Avenue from 80th to 106th Streets was recognized in 1981 for its wealth of world-class museums.

**PARK AVENUE** What is now Park Avenue was originally laid out in the 1811 Commissioners' Plan as 4th Avenue. In 1832, the long, narrow strip down the middle of the island was granted to the New York and Harlem Railroad which ran horse-drawn cars along its path starting with a run between Union Square and 23rd Street. By 1834, the service operated from Prince Street to the Upper East Side. Though given its present name in 1888, it was the 1903 conversion from steam to electric train power and the 1913 completion of the present Grand Central Terminal that paved the way for Park Avenue's classy future. The previously open rail yards and tracks were covered over by the 1920s and the avenue's wide, landscaped center medians gave credibility to its name. The rest is social registry and, later, corporate history.

Upper East Side

**PATRIARCH BARTHOLOMEW WAY** Adjacent to the Greek Orthodox Archdiocese of America, the sign honors the current Ecumenical Patriarch, world leader of all Eastern Orthodox Christians. Bartholomew is known as the Green Patriarch for his championing of environmental issues. He visited New York in 1997.

**PATRIARCH DIMITRIOS DRIVE** This honorary sign was installed in 1990 during the official visit of Patriarch Bartholomew's predecessor who died in 1991.

**RUPPERT PARK** This park and the apartment complex surrounding it are on the site of the Ruppert Brewery established here in 1867 and at one time the eighth largest in the country. Colonel Jacob Ruppert, son of the founder, was one of the early owners of the New York Yankees and was instrumental in building Yankee Stadium in the Bronx.

**SAKHAROV-BONNER CORNER** The corner of 67th Street and 3rd Avenue was named in 1984 as a tribute to Andrei Sakharov and his wife Yelena Bonner. Sakharov was a physicist in the forefront of the Soviet race to build a hydrogen bomb. Nonetheless, in 1980 he was exiled for speaking out against the Soviet government's failure to provide human rights to its citizens. Freed in 1987 by President Mikhail Gorbachev, Sakharov won a seat in the Congress of People's Deputies. He was awarded the Nobel Peace Prize in 1975 for his humanitarian efforts and died in 1989. Until its dissolution, the Soviet Mission was located just up the block, making the placement of the sign a political statement.

**TEMPLE SHAARAY TEFILA PLACE** The corner of East 79th Street and 2nd Avenue was named in 1995 in celebration of the 150th anniversary of the Shaaray Tefila congregation. The temple has been at this location since the early 1960s.

**UNITED JERUSALEM PLACE** Not far from the official residence of Israel's consul general, this sign was installed in 1990 as a gesture of support for Israel and for the effort to unite Jerusalem.

**YORK AVENUE** Originally Avenue A, the street name was changed in 1928 to honor the city's most famous World War I hero, the appropriately named Alvin C. York.

# East/Spanish Harlem

shares its history as a village, distinct and sometimes remote

from the city proper, with other enclaves—Greenwich Village,

Yorkville, Manhattanville, to cite a few—some of whose names

survive, but whose separateness and remoteness do not. The

Dutch called this village New Harlem after the old Haarlem

they had left behind in Europe. The center of the community

was situated near 125th Street on the Harlem River, though

the settlement spread across most of the northern end of the

island. Harlem was an agricultural area until the mid-19th cen-

tury when mass transportation connected the city in the south

with these northern reaches. Urbanization here took the form

predominantly of tenement construction designed to house

workers overflowing from immigrant precincts downtown. A

perusal of the street names that follow gives evidence of some

of the nationalities that have called Harlem their home in the last century. The first wave of inhabitants were German and Irish. Having attained a measure of economic security, they moved on and were replaced in the first quarter of the 20th century by Italian laborers and their families. They were later joined by Jews from eastern Europe. At about the same time, Central Harlem's African-American population was expanding east, and remains a significant presence here. Known by its dominant ethnicity as El Barrio, East Harlem is home to a Latino population of primarily Puerto Rican descent which gravitated here around the time of the First World War.

**DR. MARTIN LUTHER KING JR. BOULEVARD** Since 1984, the full length of 125th Street has honored civil rights leader and Nobel Peace Prize winner Dr. King, assassinated in 1968.

**DUKE ELLINGTON CIRCLE** The circle at 110th Street and 5th Avenue was named for this elegant and masterful musical legend in 1995. Ellington lived in several locations on the West Side of Manhattan and died here in 1974.

**EUGENE MCCABE WAY** The founder of North General Hospital is memorialized in the section of Madison Avenue that runs by it. McCabe served as president of the hospital until his death in 1998. North General is the only minority-operated hospital in New York State.

**FRAWLEY CIRCLE** Sharing the roundabout at 110th Street and 5th Avenue with the Duke Ellington tribute above, the circle was named in 1926 for James J. Frawley. A Tammany Hall district leader and state senator, Frawley's construction company built the Manhattan and Queensborough Bridges.

**FREDRICA L. TEER SQUARE** Located adjacent to the National Black Theatre, the sign recalls one of its executive directors and sister of its founder (see National Black Theatre Way below). By profession a consultant in human resources development and management training, Teer joined her sister Barbara Ann's efforts to develop the theater organization in 1975. She died in 1979, and the corner was given her name in 1994.

*Langston Hughes*

**HARLEM ART PARK** A park in Harlem for the display of art.

**HOLY ROSARY SQUARE** This commemoration was installed on the 1984 centennial of Holy Rosary Roman Catholic Church, founded to serve the Irish and German immigrants then living in East Harlem.

**LANGSTON HUGHES PLACE** The Harlem Renaissance poet and playwright made his last home at 20 East 127th Street. Hughes, 1902–1967, was an important figure in the African-American cultural blossoming in the 1920s, and the street was named for him in 1982.

**LEXINGTON AVENUE** Named in 1836 for the Revolutionary War battle of Lexington (Massachusetts), this avenue was a later addition to the Commissioners' Plan of 1811. It was laid out in 1832 in response to the need for an additional north-south artery.

**LUIS MUÑOZ MARIN BOULEVARD** A revered figure among the Puerto Rican population, Marin was a journalist and poet who became the first elected governor of that island, and went on to serve three terms. Marin fostered "Operation Bootstrap," a program under which the United States contributed millions of dollars to Puerto Rico for the development of industry and education. The sign was put up in 1982, two years after Marin died.

**MACHITO SQUARE** Named in 1985 for Cuban immigrant Frank Grillo, known as Machito. Following World War II, Grillo, who lived in Harlem, organized a band made up of black and Latino musicians called the Afro-Cubans. The band became a leading dance orchestra of the time.

**MADISON AVENUE** Like Lexington Avenue, Madison was a later addition to the 1811 Commissioners' Plan. It was opened in 1836 and named for President James Madison who died that year.

East/Spanish Harlem

135

*Marcus Garvey*

**MARCUS GARVEY PARK** Previously Mount Morris Park, this hilly green square was opened in 1840 and rechristened in 1973. Marcus Garvey, 1887–1940, instituted the Universal Negro Improvement Association, which at one time numbered two million members, and was a vehicle for the promotion of black self-sufficiency. In 1920 at Madison Square Garden, Garvey inaugurated his Pan-African movement whose goal was to set up an autonomous nation in West Africa, a destination he and his followers were to reach via his Black Star Shipping Line. Despite Garvey's positive efforts to empower his people, this last venture foundered in 1923 when Garvey was convicted of mail fraud. A unique feature of the park is a landmarked 1855 cast-iron fire watchtower, complete with a 10,000-pound bell. It is the last of its kind in the city.

**MT. CARMEL SQUARE** The 1984 centennial of Our Lady of Mount Carmel was marked by the naming of this intersection. The church is dedicated to the patron saint of the Italian village from which many area immigrants had come. Excluded from the established, predominantly Irish neighborhood churches, local Italian immigrants physically built this church themselves. Over time, the "festa" celebrated by the congregation drew more worshippers than any other church in the country, and Pope Leo XIII granted Mount Carmel the status of basilica in 1903. In observance of the remaining Italian-American population, Sunday mass is still celebrated in Italian.

**MUSEUM MILE** Fifth Avenue from 80th to 106th Streets was recognized in 1981 for its wealth of world-class museums.

**NATIONAL BLACK THEATRE WAY** The theater was founded in 1968 by Barbara Ann Teer, an actress and director. Teer's goal was to bring respect and recognition for black culture to the American theater. In 1983 the National Black Theatre initiated the National Black Institute of Communication Through Theater Arts as a way to integrate arts activities with local businesses.

**OUR LADY QUEEN OF ANGELS PLACE** The cul-de-sac on East 113th Street was named in 1990 to honor the parish established here in 1886. As with Our Lady of Mount Carmel above, this church honors the village patron saint of many local Italian-American immigrants. In the first quarter of the last century, these blocks were known as Italian Harlem with close to 90,000 residents of Italian descent.

**PALADINO AVENUE** An extension of Pleasant Avenue until the 1950s, this street curving around the Wagner Houses was renamed for Anthony C. Paladino, 1881–1944. Formalizing the street's new identity, the Proceedings of the City Council pay respect to the entire Paladino famiglia's early roots in the Italian Harlem community and their devotion to its well-being. Anthony himself, a civic leader with close ties to Governor Alfred E. Smith, was a delegate to the 1928 Democratic Presidential Convention. His construction company provided employment for many neighborhood men, particularly in times of need.

**PARK AVENUE** What is now Park Avenue was originally laid out in the 1811 Commissioners' Plan as 4th Avenue. In 1832, the long, narrow strip down the middle of the island was granted to the New York and Harlem Railroad which ran horse-drawn trains along its path starting with a run between Union Square and 23rd Street. By 1834, the service operated from Prince Street to the Upper East Side. Though given its present name in 1888, it was the 1903 conversion from steam to electric train power and the 1913 completion of the present Grand Central Terminal that paved the way for Park Avenue's classy future—at least up to 97th Street. The previously open rail yards and tracks were covered over up to this point and the avenue's wide, landscaped center medians gave credibility to its name—again, up to this point. The trains rumble in and out of their subterranean tunnel at 97th Street, their raised viaducts cleaving Park Avenue and giving the lie to its descriptive title.

**PETE PASCALE PLACE** Pascale, who died in 1997, was longtime executive director of La Guardia House, a settlement house on East 116th Street. Scores of children benefitted from Pascale's sponsoring of summer programs outside the city through the Fresh Air Fund. The street was named for this respected civic leader in 1999.

**PLEASANT AVENUE** After Avenue A on the Upper East Side was changed to York Avenue in 1928, this section of that avenue followed suit with its more evocative name.

**R. LONNIE WILLIAMS PLACE** Named in 1997 for the executive director of Boy's Harbor, an organization dedicated to empowering urban youth and their families through education, counseling, social services, and a summer camp on the east end of Long Island. Williams died in 1995.

**RONALD MCNAIR PLACE** McNair was the second African-American to travel in space and one of the seven astronauts killed on the Challenger mission in 1986. He and his family had close ties to Harlem where his father had operated an auto repair shop for 20 years.

**SYLVAN PLACE** Located in Harlem Art Park on East 120th Street, the background of this short thoroughfare's name is unknown other than as a reference to its woodsy setting.

**THOMAS JEFFERSON PARK** Acquired by the city around the turn of the century, this leafy expanse replaced six square blocks of tenements. The park is one of the few green oases in this part of the city, and is named for our third president.

TITO PUENTE WAY "Mambo King" Puente, 1923–2000, was born in Harlem and took his first music lessons in this neighborhood. East 110th Street, where he lived as a youth, was named for him shortly after his death.

TONY MENDEZ PLACE Mendez was the first East Harlem district leader of Puerto Rican extraction. Holding the office for 20 years, Mendez helped organize the first Puerto Rican Day parade and was instrumental in starting the first Boys' Club in El Barrio. Mendez died in 1982, and the street was named for him in 1989.

# West Side

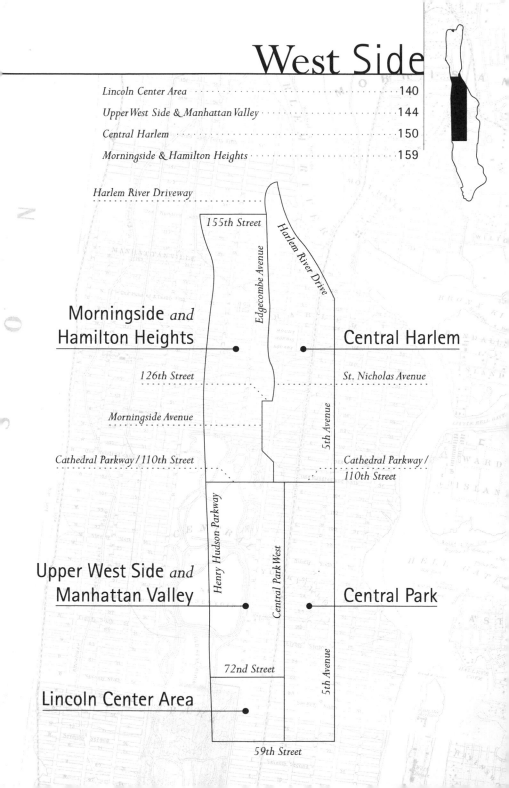

Harlem River Driveway

155th Street

*Harlem River Drive*

Edgecombe Avenue

## Morningside *and* Hamilton Heights

## Central Harlem

126th Street

St. Nicholas Avenue

Morningside Avenue

5th Avenue

Cathedral Parkway / 110th Street

Cathedral Parkway / 110th Street

Henry Hudson Parkway

Central Park West

## Upper West Side *and* Manhattan Valley

## Central Park

72nd Street

5th Avenue

## Lincoln Center Area

59th Street

# Lincoln Center Area

Lincoln Center is an example of an institution arriving, being named for, and subsuming the original name of the place in which it was constructed. Lincoln Square, though it is no longer defined by street signs, existed here nearly a century before the performing arts complex was completed which, like various other local buildings and businesses, is named for it. Unaware of the previously existing Lincoln Square, some people assume that Lincoln Center took its name from Lincoln Kirstein, co-founder of the New York City Ballet which performs in the New York State Theater here. In fact, as Lincoln Square's name was conferred in 1872, chances are good that it was chosen to recall the president who had been assassinated just seven years earlier. And, like Amsterdam and Columbus Avenues, the choice of a name evocative of a glorious figure or moment in our country's history may have been a gesture inspired less by patriotism than by marketing, and one designed to lend respectability and saleability to an area soon to be urbanized. By the time Lincoln Center was conceived, it was seen in some quarters as an antidote to the rundown tenements and stores pressed between upscale Central Park West on the east and the dismal expanse of the New York Central rail yards on the west. In the late 1950s a swath of real estate was razed for the arts center and for Fordham University's Manhattan campus. The use of the rail yards declined in the 1960s and '70s and in their place spanking new apartment buildings rose above the Hudson with views of the New Jersey Palisades. Lincoln Center is now ringed with luxury residential apartment towers, television studios, offices, schools, and an ever-changing menu of restaurants to serve the culture vultures.

ALVIN AILEY PLACE  The block where the dance company and school are located commemorates the great African-American choreographer and dancer who died in 1989.

**AMSTERDAM AVENUE** What is now Amsterdam Avenue was laid out in the 1811 Commissioners' Plan as 10th Avenue and opened from 59th Street to Fort George Avenue in 1816. The name was changed in 1890 in a bid on the part of Upper West Side landowners to confer a measure of old-world cachet to their real estate investments in an area that had yet to catch on. The new avenue name supported the speculators' claim that this section would become "the New City" and a "new, New Amsterdam."

**BROADWAY** Originally an Indian trail that ran north from the southern tip of Manhattan, Broadway now extends from the Battery into the Bronx. The street's name derives from its unusual width.

**CENTRAL PARK** In the mid-19th century the 843 acres that are now Central Park were a rough-and-tumble terrain of rocky ridges, bogs, shantytowns, and a thriving African-American community called Seneca Village perched on the western edge around 82nd Street. As the city rushed into the as yet undeveloped areas plotted for that purpose by the Commissioners' Plan, men of influence recognized that if action were not taken quickly, the opportunity to introduce parkland within the confines of the grid would be lost forever. In 1853 the city acquired the land for the park and in 1857 held a contest for its design. Frederick Law Olmsted and Calvert Vaux's "Greensward Plan," based on a Romantic English garden model, won the competition. The park opened in 1859 and on early maps is shown as "The Central Park," a nod to its central location within the city.

**COLUMBUS AVENUE** As with Amsterdam Avenue above, what was originally labeled 9th Avenue on the Commissioners' Plan was changed to the more evocative Columbus Avenue in 1890.

**DAMROSCH PARK** The corner near Lincoln Center recalls Walter Damrosch, 1862–1950, whose life was dedicated to conducting and to musical education. He was director of the Metropolitan Opera, founder of the Damrosch Opera company, and host for 14 years of a music appreciation radio show.

**FREEDOM PLACE** Three young civil rights advocates, Andrew Goodman, James Chaney, and Michael Schwerner were murdered in 1964 in Mississippi while working with the Mississippi Summer Project. This street was named in their memory in 1965.

**GEORGE BALANCHINE WAY** The great Russian-born choreographer and co-founder of the New York City Ballet died in 1983 and is honored here.

**JOHN LAWE STREET** West 64th Street between Amsterdam and West End Avenue is named for the Irish immigrant who rose from bus cleaner to fourth international president of the Transport Workers Union whose headquarters is nearby. Lawe was elected in 1977, and led the union through the 1980 11-day transit strike. He died in 1989.

West Side

**LEONARD BERNSTEIN PLACE** Bernstein, 1918–1990, conductor and music director of the New York Philharmonic Orchestra from 1958 to 1969, was the innovative and prolific composer of such world-renowned works as *West Side Story*.

**LINCOLN CENTER DRIVE NORTH** This section of West 64th Street is an access to Lincoln Center. A south access may have been planned but is nowhere in evidence.

**RICHARD TUCKER PARK** Named in 1977 for the internationally revered opera tenor known as the "American Caruso." Tucker was born in Brooklyn, debuted at the Metropolitan Opera, and died in 1975.

**RIVERSIDE BOULEVARD** Parallel to Freedom Place above, this new street is true to its name; it runs above the river, providing access to the apartment towers that replaced the New York Central rail yards and to panoramas of the New Jersey Palisades.

**SHERMAN SQUARE** A square incorporating two traffic islands where Broadway and Amsterdam intersect was named in 1891 for General William Tecumseh Sherman, legendary leader of the Union Army who died that year.

**WEST END AVENUE** Though one source asserts that the avenue took its name from the fact that the western end of the British fortifications lay along this line during the Revolution, a more likely explanation is related to the origin of Amsterdam and Columbus Avenues above. The street was laid out in the 1811 Commissioners' Plan as 11th Avenue. The name was changed to West End Avenue in 1880 at a time when West Side landowners were anxious to attract buyers to their neighborhood. A contemporary real estate publication noted that "it was the west end of all great cities which contained the finest residences and became the fashionable centre." The blocks between 59th and 110th Streets west of Central Park were called the West End during this era, and it followed naturally that the avenue's new name should capitalize on its surroundings' much-anticipated glory.

# Upper West Side & Manhattan Valley

The fact that these two areas are treated in the same section is testimony to the persistent northward movement of the city's forces of gentrification. Manhattan Valley—called SoHa by some for SOuth HArlem—is fast becoming not just an extension of the Upper West Side, but a cutting edge neighborhood, soon-to-be-taken-over-by-folks-from-downtown. Geographically, the West Side above the 50s is distinct from the flat ground to the south in that its huge rocky escarpments raise the ground level dramatically as one progresses north. Those elevations looming over the Hudson provide majestic views of the river and the New Jersey Palisades, and in the uptown heights a towering ridge soars over the tree and rooftops of the Harlem Plains. In its early history, and up until the mid-19th century, a settlement here was known as Bloomingdale, from a Dutch word meaning flower vale and recalling a town near Haarlem in the Netherlands. In the 18th century gracious country estates were built here as escapes from the nether reaches of the city. The West Side was still largely country when speculators were gobbling up the East Side. Delays in establishing transportation lines and in grading and opening streets caused the West Side to lag behind the East. Though this part of town was spared the factories and tenements that tainted the East River shore and the western sections farther south, West Side landowners struggled tirelessly to rid their properties of tenacious squatters and shantytowns. In the 1850s, anticipation that the "pleasure ground" of Central Park would spark interest in nearby property gave a boost to land speculation. The West Side Association, comprised of local property owners, waged a creative campaign to paint their sector as a new city, or an enchanting suburb of the old one. Bestowing venerable names on avenues previously identified by numbers, they sought to lure respectable buyers from settling east of the park. By 1890 the West Side land rush was in full swing, with streets and avenues in a flurry of construction. Today's version of this energy is seen in the rediscovery and renovation of the housing stock above 96th Street that happily survived the bull-dozers of urban renewal. The Upper West Side and Manhattan Valley, with their gracious ranks of row houses and august apartment buildings, have a distinct and eclectic character all their own, and manage a happy blend of homeyness and sophis-tication.

AMSTERDAM AVENUE What is now Amsterdam Avenue was laid out in the 1811 Commissioners' Plan as 10th Avenue and opened from 59th Street to Fort George Avenue in 1816. The name was changed in 1890 in a bid on the part of Upper West Side landown-ers to confer a measure of old-world cachet to their real estate investments in an area that had yet to catch on. The new avenue name supported the speculators' claim that this section would become "the New City" and a "new, New Amsterdam."

BROADWAY Originally an Indian trail that ran north from the southern tip of Manhattan, Broadway now extends from the Battery into the Bronx. The street's name derives from its unusual width.

CATHEDRAL PARKWAY The Cathedral of St. John the Divine, the namesake of this part of West 110th Street, and the largest church in the country, has been abuilding here since 1892 and continues with no end in sight.

**CENTRAL PARK** In the mid-19th century, the 843 acres that are now Central Park were a rough-and-tumble terrain of rocky ridges, bogs, shantytowns, and a thriving African-American community called Seneca Village perched on the western edge around 82nd Street. As the city rushed into the as yet undeveloped areas plotted for that purpose by the Commissioners' Plan, men of influence recognized that if action were not taken quickly, the opportunity to introduce parkland within the confines of the grid would be lost forever. In 1853 the city acquired the land for the park and in 1857 held a contest for its design. Frederick Law Olmsted and Calvert Vaux's "Greensward Plan," based on a Romantic English garden model, won the competition. The park opened in 1859 and on early maps is shown as "The Central Park," a nod to its central location within the city.

*Calvert Vaux*

**COLUMBUS AVENUE** As with Amsterdam Avenue above, what was originally labeled 9th Avenue on the Commissioners' Plan was changed to the more evocative Columbus Avenue in 1890.

*Frederick Law Olmsted*

**DUKE ELLINGTON BOULEVARD** This part of West 106th Street took the name of the elegant and masterful musical legend in 1977. Ellington lived in several locations on the West Side of Manhattan, and died here in 1974.

**EDGAR ALLAN POE STREET** The author of poems, stories, and criticism lived in Manhattan for brief periods in the mid-19th century, spending the summers of 1843 and 1844 in a farmhouse around West 84th Street. Poe moved to the Bronx in 1846 and died in 1849 in Baltimore.

*Edgar Allan Poe*

**FREDERICK DOUGLASS CIRCLE** A tribute to the former slave who used his voice and his pen in the struggle to end slavery and segregation. Douglass founded an antislavery newspaper in Rochester, New York, in 1847, discussed slavery with President Lincoln, and served as minister to Haiti from 1889 to 1891. Douglass died in 1895.

**HENRY J. BROWNE BOULEVARD** Browne, who died in 1980, was a priest attached to St. Gregory's Parish Church at 144 West 90th Street. A native of Hell's Kitchen, Browne campaigned tirelessly for low-income housing on the West Side, believing that this would protect local residents from being forced out of their neighborhoods by high-end development. Browne went on to become a professor of sociology at Rutgers University.

**ISAAC BASHEVIS SINGER BOULEVARD** This beloved author of tales of Jewish life in eastern Europe lived for many years on the Upper West Side. Singer received the Nobel Prize for literature in 1978 and died in 1991.

Upper West Side & Manhattan Valley

**JOAN OF ARC ISLAND** This little park and its equestrian statue of Joan of Arc date from 1915. The statue was unveiled on the 500th anniversary of the birth of the French national heroine, and served to honor the valiant spirit of her countrymen serving in the early years of World War I. The base of the statue incorporates stones from the Cathedral of Rheims and from the tower of Rouen, both important sites in the life of the Maid of Orléans.

**MANHATTAN AVENUE** It is possible that this avenue's name dates from the middle of the 19th century when the village of Manhattanville thrived around present-day 125th Street and Broadway. Running north-south, it is probably a vestige of the route from lower Manhattan to the village.

**POMANDER WALK** This charming group of Tudor-style row houses built in 1921 is a third generation. The grandparents are a row of houses in a suburb of London. The parents were copies of those houses used as the stage set for a popular British play that ran in New York in the early 1900s called *Pomander Walk*.

**RIVERSIDE DRIVE** Opened as far as 125th Street in 1880, this road winds sinuously along the hilly terrain above the Hudson River, splitting occasionally to embrace the upper "islands" of Riverside Park. The drive was extended at various times until 1925 when it was completed as far as Dyckman Street.

**RIVERSIDE PARK** A park designed by Olmsted and Vaux of Central Park fame had existed here since the late 19th century, but much of it had been scarred by the tracks of the New York Central Railroad. As part of the West Side Improvement Project commandeered by Robert Moses, the tracks were sunk, the park was revamped, and re-opened in 1937.

*Pomander Walk*

**STRAUS PARK**  Isidor and Ida Straus, brother and sister-in-law of Nathan (see Lower East Side), went down on the *Titanic* in 1912. This monument was created, and the little park named, in memory of the couple who lived nearby. Isidor was co-owner with his brother of R. H. Macy.

**THEODORE ROOSEVELT PARK**  The American Museum of Natural History seems a veritable tribute to our 26th president, Theodore Roosevelt, 1858–1919. Not only is the grassy lawn surrounding the museum named for him, but an imposing equestrian statue of Roosevelt stands guard on the steps at the Central Park West entrance. It is Roosevelt's contribution to the field of conservation that led to his being memorialized here. As a champion of national forests, Roosevelt established the United States Forest Service, and five new national parks. He also supported efforts to preserve wildlife.

*Theodore Roosevelt*

**VERDI SQUARE**  This traffic island honors the opera composer Giuseppe Verdi who died in 1901. Verdi's operas were interpreted as political statements supporting Italian nationalism. The statue was installed in 1906 by the Italian community of New York.

**WEST END AVENUE**  Though one source asserts that the avenue took its name from the fact that the western end of the British fortifications lay along this line during the Revolution, a more likely explanation is related to the origin of Amsterdam and Columbus Avenues above. The street was laid out in the Commissioners' Plan as 11th Avenue. The name was changed to West End Avenue in 1880 at a time when West Side landowners were anxious to attract buyers to their neighborhood. A contemporary real estate publication noted that "it was the west end of all great cities which contained the finest residences and became the fashionable centre." The blocks between 59th and 110th Streets west of Central Park were called the West End during this era and it followed naturally that the avenue's new name should capitalize on its surroundings' much-anticipated glory.

# Central Harlem With its broad

boulevards sweeping for miles north of Central Park, the great

mid-island corridor of Manhattan that is Central Harlem is

impressive in its expanse. Banked up against the rocky promon-

tories of Morningside and Hamilton Heights on the west, and

running flat to the East and Harlem Rivers on the east,

Harlem's geography gave rise to its early, descriptive titles of

Harlem Plain or Harlem Valley. Prior to the mid-19th century,

the northern sector of Manhattan was characterized by scat-

tered farms, shantytowns, estates, and villages. After the Civil

War, St. Nicholas Avenue was a favorite racing ground for the

moneyed set to display their pedigreed steeds. As elsewhere,

change was wrought by the introduction of mass transporta-

tion to the area, particularly the elevated trains in the late

1870s which prompted a surge in speculative homebuilding.

Unlike East Harlem, the market for housing here was

predominantly middle to upper-middle class. Both native-born and European—mostly German Jews—made their homes here, a fact that accounts for the abundance of amply proportioned and richly detailed row houses which survive from that era, including Striver's Row on 138th and 139th Streets. What the "els" had done in the 1870s, the construction of subways continued and extended just a generation later, but with a difference. This time, housing speculation, mostly in the northern section of Harlem, focused on tenement building for a whole new population. Ironically, the transportation explosion succeeded too well to benefit Harlem, and the tenants for whom these apartment buildings were intended stayed on the train, and found cheaper housing even farther north in newly accessible outer neighborhoods or beyond the city altogether. The resulting Harlem housing glut opened the door for owners to admit a previously unacceptable population. Suddenly money from African-American wallets was welcome, and Harlem became a magnet for black city dwellers. This development coincided and interrelated with two others: the Great Migration of blacks from the American South and the Caribbean, and the Harlem Renaissance. Fleeing racial and economic discrimination in the regions of their birth, huge numbers of African-Americans sought better conditions in the north, with thousands settling in Harlem. The stage was thus set for a cultural movement inspired by the leadership of such black intellectuals as W. E. B. Du Bois, James Weldon Johnson, and Alain Locke, who called upon their people to appreciate themselves as proud, creatively gifted descendants of a glorious African heritage—in short a "New Negro." The brief but widely influential cultural flowering of the Harlem Renaissance produced works in nearly every field of art, and was brought to a close by the Depression. Since that time the whole gamut of social evils so well chronicled in the press has visited Harlem and has devastated parts of it. Surprisingly, Harlem's woes have left it in a position to reap the benefits of a whole new renaissance—this one centered on real estate. During its down years little renewal occurred in this section. The spacious row houses built at the end of the 19th century were left in place, many relatively intact. With Manhattan housing prices shooting through the stratosphere, and buyers falling over each other to snatch up "bargains" uptown, Harlem is enjoying a boom that should bring the bloom back to its stately boulevards.

ADAM CLAYTON POWELL JR. BLVD. The name of 7th Avenue north of Central Park was changed in 1974, two years after the death of the flamboyant pastor of Harlem's Abyssinian Baptist Church. Powell Jr. assumed the mantle from his father, Adam Clayton Powell, Sr., who, in his zeal for black New Yorkers to move to Harlem, relocated his parish from West 40th to West 138th Street. Powell Jr., a civil rights leader, served 11 terms in the House of Representatives, and was the first black member of the City Council. After losing his seat in Congress, winning it back and refusing to take it, Powell retired to the island of Bimini. He died in 1972.

AFRICAN SQUARE To recognize this intersection of 125th Street as the scene of speeches by revered African-American leaders such as Malcolm X, Adam Clayton Powell, Jr., W. E. B. Du Bois, and Marcus Garvey, this name was bestowed in 1983. The naming also acknowledges 125th Street as the heart of the Harlem community.

A. PHILIP RANDOLPH SQUARE Named for Admiral George Dewey in 1922, the square was renamed in 1964 for Randolph, a labor and civil rights leader who was president of the Brotherhood of Sleeping Car Porters founded by him in 1925, and of the Negro American Labor Council. Randolph also organized the 1942 march on Washington which demanded an end to racial discrimination in defense industries.

Central Harlem

**BISHOP R. C. LAWSON PLACE** Lawson founded the Church of Our Lord Jesus Christ of the Apostolic Faith on West 124th Street in 1919.

**BLESSED EDMUND RICE STREET** The Irish founder of the Congregation of Christian Brothers teaching order is honored on a block of West 124th Street where the Brothers have started three schools. Rice lived from 1762 to 1844, and has been beatified, the first step toward sainthood.

**BRADHURST AVENUE** Named for Dr. Samuel Bradhurst, an 18th-century New York physician whose home, or country house, stood near here. Bradhurst left the property to his son John, a druggist, who held it until 1845.

**CATHEDRAL PARKWAY** The Cathedral of St. John the Divine, the namesake of this part of West 110th Street, and the largest church in the country, has been abuilding here since 1892 and continues with no end in sight.

**CHISUM PLACE** This short street named in 1961 provides access to the North Harlem Houses apartment complex. Adjacent to the armory of the 369th Infantry Regiment (see 369th Plaza below), the street honors Colonel W. Woodruff Chisum, commander of the regiment which served from its New York base during World War II.

**COLONEL CHARLES YOUNG TRIANGLE** Young, 1864–1922, a graduate of West Point and a veteran of the Spanish-American War, was appointed military attaché to Haiti in 1906, and to Liberia in 1912. This little park was named for Young in 1937.

**DORRANCE BROOKS SQUARE** The first public square to be named for an African-American soldier, this one was designated in 1925 to memorialize a private in the 15th Infantry who was killed in World War I (see 369th Plaza below).

**DR. MARTIN LUTHER KING BOULEVARD** Since 1984, the full length of 125th Street has honored civil rights leader and Nobel Peace Prize winner Dr. King, assassinated in 1968.

**DUKE ELLINGTON CIRCLE** The circle at 110th Street and 5th Avenue was named for this elegant and masterful musical legend in 1995. Ellington lived in several locations on the West Side of Manhattan, and died here in 1974.

**EDGECOMBE AVENUE** Call it a cliff, a rocky precipice, or a combe, this avenue runs along it—the one looming over Jackie Robinson Park, that is. The street was opened in 1811, but named sometime later to conjure up its picturesque qualities for potential home builders.

*Duke Ellington*

**ESPLANADE GARDENS PLAZA**  The northern end of Lenox Avenue takes its name from the apartment complex on the adjacent blocks.

**FRAWLEY CIRCLE**  Sharing the roundabout at 110th Street and 5th Avenue with the Duke Ellington tribute above, the circle was named in 1926 for James J. Frawley. A Tammany Hall district leader and state senator, Frawley's construction company built the Manhattan and Queensborough Bridges.

**FREDERICK DOUGLASS BOULEVARD & CIRCLE**  A tribute to the former slave who used his voice and his pen in the struggle to end slavery and segregation. Douglass founded an antislavery newspaper in Rochester, New York, in 1847, discussed slavery with President Lincoln, and served as minister to Haiti from 1889 to 1891. Douglass died in 1895.

**FREDRICA L. TEER SQUARE**  Located adjacent to the National Black Theatre, the sign recalls one of its executive directors and sister of its founder (see National Black Theatre Way below). By profession a consultant in human resources development and management training, Teer joined her sister Barbara Ann's efforts to develop the theater organization in 1975. She died in 1979, and the corner was given her name in 1994.

**HANCOCK PLACE & PARK**  These sites recall Winfield Scott Hancock, 1824–1886, a Union general in the Civil War during which he fought in the battles of Antietam, Chancellorsville, Gettysburg, and the Wilderness. In 1880, the Democrats nominated him for president, but he lost to James A. Garfield.

**HARLEM RIVER DRIVEWAY**  This access road to the Harlem River Drive is a vestige of its precursor, the Harlem Speedway, which opened in 1898 (see Perimeter Routes).

**HARLEM RIVER PARK**  A tiny grassy plot adjoining the Harlem River Drive at East 127th Street.

**JACKIE ROBINSON PARK**  This verdant strip of park was previously known as Colonial Park but was renamed in 1978 for the great second baseman and hitter who, when he joined the Brooklyn Dodgers in 1947, made history for breaking the color barrier in organized baseball. Born in Georgia in 1919, Robinson died in 1972.

*Jackie Robinson*

**LAFAYETTE SQUARE**  Somewhere along the line, this little square lost the first part of its name. The land for Washington-Lafayette Square was acquired by the city in 1887. In 1900, Charles Broadway Rouss presented to the city the statue of George Washington and the Marquis de Lafayette—French hero of the Revolution—shaking hands. The statue had been crafted by Frédéric-Auguste Bartholdi, sculptor of the Statue of Liberty.

*James Lenox*

**LENOX AVENUE** James Lenox was the son of the Robert Lenox for whom Lenox Hill on the Upper East Side is named. James was a collector of works of art and books. His library, combined with that of John Jacob Astor and with a trust left by Samuel J. Tilden, established the New York Public Library. This part of 6th Avenue above Central Park was named for Lenox in 1887.

**LENOX AVENUE/MALCOLM X BOULEVARD & PLAZA** In 1987, Lenox Avenue was given an additional, commemorative title. The new name recognizes the Black Muslim leader who was assassinated in 1965.

**LENOX TERRACE PLACE** A short street giving access to the Lenox Terrace apartment complex on West 135th Street.

**LLOYD E. DICKENS PLACE** A successful real estate broker and groundbreaking force in Harlem's economic growth, Dickens, who died in 1988, is celebrated on the block where he first lived in Harlem. Dickens was a powerful voice in Democratic politics for over 40 years, was active in numerous civic activities promoting Harlem's development, and is credited as a role model for younger African-Americans who followed him into the public arena.

**MACOMB PLACE** In 1813 Robert Macomb built a dam across the Harlem River at about 155th Street in order to provide power for a mill on the Bronx shore. The dam blocked traffic on the river, and was destroyed in 1838. The bridge that crosses to the Bronx at this point bears Macomb's name.

**MANHATTAN AVENUE** It is possible that this avenue's name dates from the middle of the 19th century when the village of Manhattanville thrived around present-day 125th Street and Broadway. Running north-south, it is probably a vestige of the route from lower Manhattan to the village.

**MARCUS GARVEY PARK** Previously Mount Morris Park, this hilly green square was opened in 1840 and rechristened in 1973. Marcus Garvey, 1887–1940, instituted the Universal Negro Improvement Association, which at one time numbered two million members, and was a vehicle for the promotion of black self-sufficiency. In 1920 at Madison Square Garden, Garvey inaugurated his Pan-African Movement whose goal was to set up an autonomous nation in West Africa, a destination he and his followers were to reach via his Black Star Shipping Line. Despite Garvey's positive efforts to empower his people, this last venture foundered in 1923 when Garvey was convicted of mail fraud. A unique feature of the park is a landmarked 1855 cast-iron fire watchtower, complete with a 10,000-pound bell. It is the last of its kind in the city.

**MARY MCLEOD BETHUNE PLACE** Among the trail-blazing African-American women to leave their names inscribed in Harlem history is Bethune, 1875–1955, who, among a host of other endeavors, masterminded the National Council of Negro Women in 1935, served on the National Child Welfare Commission under Presidents Coolidge and Hoover, and was advisor to President Franklin Delano Roosevelt on the Federal Council on Negro Affairs. Public School 92, named for Bethune, is on this block.

*Mary McLeod Bethune*

**MATTHEW S. TURNER TRIANGLE** The triangle was named in 1993 for this longtime member of Community Board No. 10 who co-founded the Harlem Youth Federation, advocating for education, recreation, and freedom from drugs for Harlem youth.

**MORNINGSIDE AVENUE AND PARK** The park acquired its epithet in the last quarter of the 19th century. The name is descriptive, referring literally to the light of the morning sun which sets the high cliffs aglow before illuminating the valley below. The park was designed by Frederick Law Olmsted and Calvert Vaux of Central Park fame and opened in 1887. The avenue and neighborhood (to be discussed in the next section) take their names from the park.

**MOUNT MORRIS PARK WEST** Opened in 1840, this area was called Mount Morris Square and was centered on a dramatic, forested outcropping of rock (now Marcus Garvey Park). As levelling this geological formation for housing development was deemed imprac-ticable, it was decided to leave it as a park. The origin of the name is a puzzle. It may be for Robert H. Morris, mayor of the city from 1841 to 1844, but this is doubtful, as the name appears on maps before Morris took office. The Morris family owned huge tracts of land in the Bronx, but none documented in this neighborhood. Perhaps this park got its name from the good view it affords of the Morris land across the river.

**NATIONAL BLACK THEATRE WAY** The theater was founded in 1968 by Barbara Ann Teer, an actress and director. Teer's goal was to bring respect and recognition for black cul-ture to the American theater. In 1983, the National Black Theatre initiated the National Black Institute of Communication Through Theater Arts as a way to integrate arts activities with local businesses.

**ODELL M. CLARK PLACE** Clark was a laundry worker who, dissatisfied with poor working conditions in this industry, organized the Amalgamated Laundry Workers in 1938. He was a deacon of the Abyssinian Baptist Church for 30 years, worked for Adam Clayton Powell, Jr., investigating discrimination against blacks, and died in 1980.

**REVEREND JOHN P. LADSON PLACE**  The Second Canaan Missionary Baptist Church was organized by Reverend Ladson in 1947 who served as its pastor for 35 years.

**ST. NICHOLAS AVENUE**  The Dutch settlers in New Amsterdam celebrated St. Nicholas Day in December as they had done in their homeland. Washington Irving, author of the fictional *Knickerbocker's History of New York*, is credited with re-popularizing the tradition in 19th-century New York by pronouncing St. Nicholas the patron saint of the city. The avenue was laid out in 1866 on the path of the Albany Post Road.

**SAMUEL MARX TRIANGLE**  Marx was a prominent auctioneer and appraiser who was also a Tammany leader for the 31st Assembly District. He lived in this neighborhood and died in 1922.

*Washington Irving*

**SUGAR RAY ROBINSON CORNER**  The corner was named in 1989 for the boxing legend who grew up in Harlem and who had died that year. Robinson's real name was Walker Smith, Jr. He "borrowed" the name of another fighter whose Amateur Athletic Union card he used in order to be eligible for a fight.

**369TH PLAZA**  The yellow street sign at 142nd Street and 5th Avenue stands in front of the 369th Regiment Armory, home of the Harlem Hellfighters, a celebrated all-black regiment from New York City that fought valiantly in World War I. The armory remains the headquarters of the 369th Corps, Support Battalion, New York National Guard.

**WESLEY WILLIAMS PLACE**  This part of West 135th Street commemorates one of the city's first African-American firefighters. Williams's career began in 1919, and though subjected to protests both from within the department and outside, he advanced to become the first black battalion chief.

# Morningside & Hamilton Heights

A thumbnail sketch of this district's history can be gleaned from the number of streets whose names bear witness to the many institutions which have gravitated here. Upper Manhattan's exaggerated geological contours made it ineligible for the relentless clearing and leveling that befell the less dramatic landscape farther south. Defined by plateaus and valleys, it is reminiscent of the island's original state. Even Central Park, though it looks natural and in places wild, is the result of a total topographical reconfiguration designed to appeal to a specific aesthetic. In the 18th century, the well-to-do sought the clean, cool air of the Heights neighborhoods for their country estates. In the early 19th century, Morningside also afforded open space and privacy for the Bloomingdale Insane Asylum, whose very presence here deterred interest in the surrounding real estate. A delay in extending mass transportation to these remote areas was also a contributing factor to its continued isolation. Eventually, however, the pressures of urbanization prevailed. By 1891 the asylum had sold out and a new era of institutional life began for Morningside. Beginning in 1887, the following institutions established themselves in these precincts: the Cathedral of St. John the Divine, St. Luke's Hospital, Columbia College, Teachers College, Riverside Church, Barnard College, Union and Jewish Theological Seminaries, and the Institute of Musical Art, later known as Juilliard. The term "acropolis" used at the time to characterize this section was not far off the mark. When public transit finally reached here in the form of a subway under Broadway, residential construction followed quickly, predominantly in the form of apartment buildings. Hamilton Heights, just to the north, was the site of Alexander Hamilton's country home where he lived from 1802 until his death in a duel with Aaron Burr in 1804. Again, residential development followed transportation, and in the early 20th century elegant houses filled the blocks around Hamilton's "Grange." From the 1920s to 1950s, Sugar Hill, a grouping of houses on blocks from 145th to 149th Streets, was home to many celebrated black figures—Thurgood Marshall and Zora Neale Hurston among others. Starting in the 1940s, the district's population shifted from white to black and Latino, with a large Dominican contingent. Hamilton Heights has its own institutional presence in the campuses of City College, and while the view from the College over the tree tops of St. Nicholas Park to Harlem below may not be the rooftops of Paris, it runs a close second.

ADOLPH LEWISOHN PLAZA This street on the campus of City College honors the benefactor who provided funding for a stadium—now demolished—named for him. Lewisohn, 1849–1938, along with his brothers Leonard and Julius, was a copper magnate at the end of the 19th century.

ALPHONSO B. DEAL STREET Born in 1946, Deal was instrumental in the founding of the New York State Commission on Minorities. Having been a senior New York State Supreme Court clerk, he helped develop and operate an NAACP-sponsored training program to assist minority applicants take the state court officers' examination. Deal was president of the West 140th Street Block Association, hence the street's being named for him in 1990. He died in 1988.

**AMSTERDAM AVENUE**   What is now Amsterdam Avenue was laid out in the Commissioners' Plan as 10th Avenue and opened from 59th Street to Fort George Avenue in 1816. The name was changed in 1890 in a bid on the part of Upper West Side landowners to confer a measure of old-world cachet to their real estate investments in an area that had yet to catch on. The new avenue name supported the speculators' claim that this section would become "the New City" and a "new, New Amsterdam."

**BROADWAY**   Originally an Indian trail that ran north from the southern tip of Manhattan, Broadway now extends from the Battery into the Bronx. The street's name derives from its unusual width.

**CATHEDRAL PARKWAY**   The Cathedral of St. John the Divine, the namesake of this part of West 110th Street, and the largest church in the country, has been abuilding here since 1892 and continues with no end in sight.

**CLAREMONT AVENUE**   The avenue name is the only remnant of an estate located here in the early 19th century belonging to a Michael Hogan. One source notes that Hogan was a native of County Clare in Ireland which led him to christen his property "Claremont."

**CONVENT AVENUE**   Starting in the mid-19th century, the Society of the Sacred Heart was located approximately where the south campus of City College is now. The society consisted of 10 academic buildings including Manhattanville College of the Sacred Heart which later relocated to Westchester. The avenue takes its name from this group of institutions.

**CONVENT GARDEN**   This charming traffic island-cum-garden is named for its location on Convent Avenue.

**DONNELLAN SQUARE**   This is a small square with a large spelling problem. A record exists of the World War I death of a Joseph John Donnellon (note spelling of last syllable) who had lived nearby at 480 Convent Avenue. In the same conflict a Timothy Donnellan died, but the records provide no address. To further complicate the issue, current atlases of Manhattan show this spot as Donnelson Square.

**DR. MARTIN LUTHER KING JR. BOULEVARD**   Since 1984 the full length of 125th Street has honored civil rights leader and Nobel Peace Prize winner Dr. King, assassinated in 1968.

**EDGECOMBE AVENUE**   Call it a cliff, a rocky precipice, or a combe, this avenue runs along it—the one looming over Jackie Robinson Park, that is. The street was opened in 1811, but named sometime later to conjure up its picturesque qualities for potential home builders.

**FIREFIGHTERS LAWRENCE FITZPATRICK & GERALD FRISBY CORNER**   One trying to rescue the other, these two young firefighters died in a 1980 fire nearby.

FREDERICK DOUGLASS CIRCLE A tribute to the former slave who used his voice and his pen in the struggle to end slavery and segregation. Douglass founded an antislavery newspaper in Rochester, New York, in 1847, discussed slavery with President Lincoln, and served as minister to Haiti from 1889 to 1891. Douglass died in 1895.

HAMILTON TERRACE & PLACE Named for Alexander Hamilton, 1755–1804. Hamilton, a lawyer who had been a delegate to the Continental Congress and the Constitutional Convention, was the new republic's first secretary of the Treasury. Hamilton occupied his country home, Hamilton Grange, located here on Convent Avenue at 141st Street, until his death in a duel with Aaron Burr.

*Frederick Douglass*

JOHNNY HARTMAN PLAZA The plaque that memorializes him in this shady traffic island lauds Hartman as "A musical giant in the field of jazz." Hartman was a Grammy-nominated jazz singer who sang with Dizzy Gillespie, John Coltrane, and Earl Hines. He died in 1983.

KOSSUTH ISLAND On Riverside Drive between 110th and 113th Streets, this diminutive park features a statue of Lajos Kossuth, 1802–1894. A Hungarian political reformer, Kossuth is revered for his leadership in his country's drive for independence from Austria in the 1840s. Kossuth visited the United States after fleeing Hungary, and his statue remains an important symbol for Hungarian-Americans.

*Alexander Hamilton*

LASALLE STREET Jean Baptiste de la Salle, 1651–1719, was the founder of the Institute of the Brothers of the Christian Schools, a Catholic teaching order devoted to the education of boys. This street, named in 1920, is a reminder of Manhattan College, established at 131st Street and Broadway in 1853 by la Salle's order. The name of the college was chosen to avoid giving any indication of its Catholic origin because at the time, members of the anti-immigration Know-Nothing Party destroyed institutions smacking of foreign influence. The college moved to the Bronx in 1923.

MONTEFIORE PARK Before it moved to the Bronx in 1913, Montefiore Hospital was located near this park. The hospital was founded to care for terminally ill, indigent Jews. Its name honors Moses Montefiore, a sheriff of London.

**MORNINGSIDE DRIVE & PARK** The drive and the neighborhood take their epithets from Morningside Park which acquired it in the last quarter of the 19th century. The name is descriptive, referring literally to the light of the morning sun which sets the high cliffs aglow before illuminating the valley below. The park was designed by Frederick Law Olmsted and Calvert Vaux, creators of Central Park, and opened in 1887.

**OLD BROADWAY** The two little stretches of street running at odd angles off Broadway are the last vestiges of the original course taken by Broadway in its early days as an Indian trail. The trail was used by European settlers to reach the northern part of the island. This part of it became known as the Bloomingdale Road, as it ran through the village of that name.

**REINHOLD NIEBUHR PLACE** Niebuhr, 1892–1971, was a Protestant theologian and professor at neighboring Union Theological Seminary. This portion of West 120th Street received his name in 1976.

**REVEREND DR. JOHN W. SAUNDERS PLACE** The Convent Avenue Baptist Church was founded and led by Reverend Saunders. He died in 1961.

**RIVERSIDE DRIVE** Opened as far as 125th Street in 1880, this road winds sinuously along the hilly terrain above the Hudson River, splitting occasionally to embrace the upper "islands" of Riverside Park. The drive was extended at various times until 1925 when it was completed as far as Dyckman Street.

**RIVERSIDE PARK** A park designed by Olmsted and Vaux of Central Park fame had existed here since the late 19th century, but much of it had been scarred by the tracks of the New York Central Railroad. As part of the West Side Improvement Project commandeered by Robert Moses, the tracks were sunk, the park was revamped, and re-opened in 1937.

**ROOSEVELT TRIANGLE** This sculpture island commemorates Theodore Roosevelt, 1858–1919. Roosevelt was the only native of New York City to become president. Prior to that he served as president of the New York City Board of Police Commissioners, and as assistant secretary of the navy. In 1898 he led the Rough Riders in the Spanish-American War, and was elected governor of New York State. Following the assassination of William McKinley, Roosevelt, at the time vice president, assumed the presidency and was in office from 1901 to 1909. He died in 1919.

**ST. CLAIR PLACE** In 1797 five-year-old St. Clair Pollack died from a fall on the rocks along the river here. Both his grave, which can still be seen here, and the street name preserve his memory.

**ST. MARY'S PLACE** Named for St. Mary's Protestant Episcopal Church founded in 1824 on West 126th Street between Old Broadway and Amsterdam Avenue in what was the village of Manhattanville.

**ST. NICHOLAS AVENUE & TERRACE** The Dutch settlers in New Amsterdam celebrated St. Nicholas Day in December as they had done in their homeland. Washington Irving, author of the fictional *Knickerbocker's History of New York,* is credited with having re-popularized the tradition in 19th-century New York by pronouncing St. Nicholas the patron saint of the city. The avenue was laid out in 1866 on the path of the Albany Post Road.

**ST. NICHOLAS PARK** The land for the park was acquired by the city starting in 1885, and it was designed by Samuel Parsons. The naming is consistent with the entry above.

**SAKURA PARK** Formerly Claremont Park, the new name was given to acknowledge the gift in 1912 of 2,000 cherry trees from Japan to New York City. The trees were planted here and in Riverside Park. Sakura is the Japanese word for cherry blossom.

**SEMINARY ROW** In 1986 this designation was added to West 122nd Street on the 150th anniversary of Union Theological Seminary and the 100th anniversary of the Jewish Theological Seminary.

**SHONA BAILEY PLACE** Shona was a 21-year-old aspiring actress and Girl Scout leader who was murdered in her home. The corner was named for her in 1993.

**TIEMANN PLACE** Daniel F. Tiemann was mayor of the city in 1858 and a vestryman and warden of nearby St. Mary's Protestant Episcopal Church. His paint and ink factory was located in this neighborhood.

**VINEGAR HILL CORNER** The archivist of City College reports that the February 26, 1969 issue of the *Campus,* the college's student newspaper (and incidentally the oldest continuously published student publication in the United States), featured an article on Vinegar Hill, the last Irish bar in the neighborhood at 135th Street and Amsterdam Avenue. The article was an interview with a gentleman called "Mr." who identified himself as the last Irishman in the neighborhood. Vinegar Hill was the name of a 1798 battle during a rebellion in Ireland and though Hamilton Heights is not known as an Irish community, Irish workers were employed by the thousands in building the Croton Aqueduct which ran down Amsterdam Avenue until it was buried under that avenue in the 1860s. It would follow that some of the workers settled in the vicinity of their work. Additionally, the Catholic Manhattan College was located at 131st and Broadway until 1923, and the campus of the Society of the Sacred Heart was at 135th and Convent Avenue. The 1998 City Council proceedings naming this corner state only that it was named in recognition of the diverse area's strong sense of community. Given the above conditions, it would not be surprising if the bar's name were a vestige of a staunch Irish population from an earlier era.

# Upper Manhattan

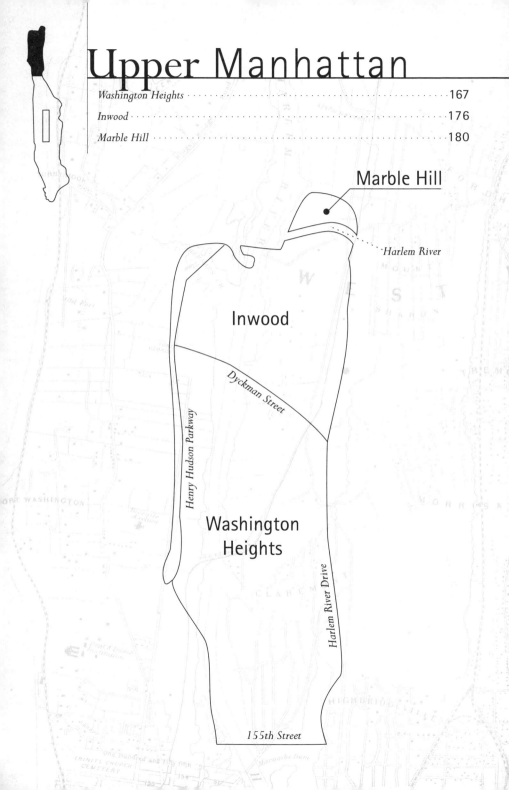

Marble Hill

Harlem River

Inwood

Dyckman Street

Henry Hudson Parkway

Washington Heights

Harlem River Drive

155th Street

# Washington Heights That

geography is destiny can be said equally of the southern and

the northern tips of Manhattan. Each pole's physical charac-

teristics and location have ordained that it will play a pivotal

role in guarding the island from unwanted or hostile incursions

from without. The south end is uniquely formed and situated

to screen travelers from the sea, while the extreme topogra-

phy of the north defends against invasion by land. The names

attached to streets and places in Washington Heights reflect

this dramatic landscape and tell a story of early Dutchmen put-

ting down roots and seeds in clearings wrested from the native

denizens. Others recall peaceful burghers plying their trades in

the service of establishing a viable community. Bastions of the

Revolution and their beleaguered leaders, Civil War heroes,

and World War I fatalities swell the roll call here. The Heights'

remote location foiled development from downtown until the

early part of the last century, thereby preserving both its rural character and its historic place names. In the 18th and 19th centuries, these hilly regions afforded attractive sites for country estates. Urbanization, when it did come, followed the opening of the Broadway subway line in 1906. Apartment complexes followed quickly as did a multitude of ethnicities to fill them. At this writing, Washington Heights is home to the city's largest Dominican population, and the lively "marqueta" atmosphere along St. Nicholas Avenue contrasts merrily with the august monoliths of Columbia-Presbyterian Medical Center and the spartan blocks of Yeshiva University. Long strips of park border the Heights on both flanks, and unexpected pockets of greenery nestle amid its quieter thoroughfares. Though gashed by the island-wide approach to the George Washington Bridge, Washington Heights is bound together by its rich history, geography, and social diversity.

**ALEX ROSE PLACE**  Born in Warsaw in 1898, Rose was a former milliner who went on to become president of the United Hatters, Cap & Millinery Workers Union. Rose was one of the 1944 founders of the Liberal Party, and a party leader until his death in 1976. Termed a political kingmaker, Rose was instrumental in bringing Fiorello La Guardia and John Lindsay to City Hall, and was involved with Presidents Franklin Roosevelt, Truman, Kennedy, and Johnson. He lived at 200 Cabrini Boulevard.

**AMSTERDAM AVENUE**  What is now Amsterdam Avenue was laid out in the 1811 Commissioners' Plan as 10th Avenue and opened from 59th Street to Fort George Avenue in 1816. The name was changed in 1890 in a bid on the part of Upper West Side landowners to confer a measure of old-world cachet to their real estate investments in an area that had yet to catch on. The new avenue name supported the speculators' claim that this section would become "the New City" and a "new, New Amsterdam."

*John James Audubon*

**ARDEN STREET**  The land surrounding this street had been owned by a pre-Revolutionary butcher named Jacob Arden.

**AUDUBON AVENUE**  Naturalist and painter John James Audubon, 1785–1851, was born in Haiti but came to live in New York City, acquiring an estate in the vicinity of 155th Street and the Hudson River. Part of the property which he sold off is now Trinity Cemetery where Audubon is buried.

**BENNETT AVENUE & PARK**  The avenue and park are named for *New York Herald* founder James Gordon Bennett, 1795–1872, whose country estate was situated here. James Gordon Bennett, Jr. donated the park to the city in 1903 in memory of his father.

**BOGARDUS PLACE**  The Dutch immigrant Bogardus family owned a large property in this locale. A member of this family, James Bogardus, 1800–1874, was an inventor, engineer, and architect who developed designs allowing whole buildings to be constructed of cast iron. He was a major influence in the city's boom in cast-iron buildings best seen preserved in SoHo.

**BROADWAY**  Originally an Indian trail that ran north from the southern tip of Manhattan, Broadway now extends from the Battery into the Bronx. The street's name derives from its unusual width.

**BROADWAY TERRACE**  A short dogleg street on a hillside above Broadway at about 193rd Street.

Washington Heights

CABRINI BOULEVARD  Mother Francis Xavier Cabrini was a missionary who emigrated from Italy to the U.S. in 1889 and became a religious leader for Italian immigrants. Cabrini traveled widely in this country and founded 67 educational institutions, orphanages, and hospitals here, in Europe, and in Central and South America. She was the first American citizen to be canonized by the Roman Catholic Church. The Missionary Sisters of the Sacred Heart, an order begun by Cabrini, opened Cabrini High School on Fort Washington Boulevard. Cabrini's remains are entombed in the school's chapel.

CHITTENDEN AVENUE  Lucius Chittenden was a merchant from New Orleans. He bought the tract of land through which the street runs in 1846, and built his home there.

COLONEL ROBERT MAGAW PLACE  Magaw was in command of Fort Washington—a footprint of which remains in nearby Bennett Park—during the Revolutionary War. He bravely resisted but ultimately surrendered the fort to the British in November of 1776. The capture of Magaw's forces cleared Manhattan of American forces and the island was occupied by the British for the next seven years.

DAVID B. FRIEDLAND SQUARE  Friedland was a lawyer and member of the City Council from Washington Heights-Inwood from 1965 until his death in 1976.

DONGAN PLACE  Named for Thomas Dongan, appointed British colonial governor of New York by James, Duke of York, in 1682. It was Dongan, 1634–1715, who gave the city its first charter, subdivided the city into wards, and created the Common Council, precursor of today's City Council.

DYCKMAN STREET  Jan Dyckman was one of the original property owners in Harlem, and bought land near the northern tip of the island in 1677. The Dyckman holdings in the area grew to be extensive.

EDGECOMBE AVENUE  Call it a cliff, a rocky precipice, or a combe, this avenue runs along it—the one looming over Highbridge Park, that is. The street was opened in 1811, but named sometime later to conjure up its picturesque qualities for potential home builders.

EDWARD M. MORGAN PLACE  Morgan, hailed as "the best post office man in the country," became postmaster of New York City in 1897. He died in 1925 and this honor was bestowed the following year.

ELLWOOD STREET  There is no known derivation for the name of this street.

FAIRVIEW AVENUE  This street does indeed afford a fair view as it winds its way down from the heights of Fort George Avenue.

FORT GEORGE AVENUE & HILL  In 1776, the American rebel forces erected a fort on Laurel Hill located approximately where today's Audubon and Fort George Avenues intersect. The British captured it and named it Fort George in honor of their king.

**FORT TRYON PARK** The park takes its name from Revolutionary War battlements erected by the Americans, seized by Hessian and British forces, and named by them for Sir William Tryon, the last British governor of the colony. Following in his father's footsteps, Frederick Law Olmsted, Jr. designed the park which opened in 1935. Three years later, the Cloisters, the medieval showcase of the Metropolitan Museum of Art, was established in the park.

**FORT WASHINGTON AVENUE & PARK** Named for George Washington and recalling the site of the Battle of Fort Washington which took place in 1776 (see Colonel Robert Magaw Place above). An outline of the fort remains in Bennett Park. The British capture of the fort cleared Manhattan of American forces and the island was occupied by the British for the next seven years.

*George Washington*

**GEORGE WASHINGTON BRIDGE PARK** A little park overlooking the big bridge.

**GORMAN PARK** The city came into the ownership of this hilly little park by default. Gertrude Emily Gorman Webb, who died in 1923, owned the land. Her will left her estate to her husband, Charles Webb, with instructions that this parcel be laid out as a park with a memorial staircase in honor of Gertrude's deceased mother, Emilie A. Gorman. Litigation over the probation of the will and over Gertrude's rights as executor of her mother's will so depleted the estate that Mr. Webb, in order to comply with his wife's desires, gave the land to the city with an endowment for its upkeep, and with the stipulation that it be maintained as a memorial to Gertrude Emily Gorman Webb and her mother.

**HAVEN AVENUE** John A. Haven bought property here starting in 1834. The street bearing his name cuts through the parcel that belonged to him and his family. The Havens' house stood just south of 181st Street, and survived until the early years of the 20th century.

**HENSHAW STREET** The World War I *Roll of Honor* lists John G. Henshaw of this neighborhood who died of bronchial pneumonia and influenza during that war in 1918.

**HIGHBRIDGE PARK** The park running along the Harlem River Drive is the Manhattan footing for the High Bridge, one of the oldest bridges in the city. Part of the Croton Aqueduct System bringing water to Manhattan, the bridge was originally constructed in the 1840s. The land for the park was acquired incrementally from 1849 to 1906. It was designed by Samuel Parsons, Jr. and Calvert Vaux, and was opened in 1888.

**HILLSIDE AVENUE** Another descriptive street name arising from the dramatic local geography, this one too lives up to its depiction.

*Jumel Mansion*

**J. HOOD WRIGHT PARK** Wright, 1835–1894, at the time of his death was a member of the firm of Drexel, Morgan & Co., and a well-known banker and railroad reorganizer. He died from "a stroke of apoplexy" while waiting for an elevated train from work to his home, a large stone residence called "The Folly" which stood in the current park. Wright's will left $100,000 to what is now the Washington Heights Branch of the New York Public Library, stipulating that it change from a subscription to a free library, and $580,000 to the Manhattan Dispensary Hospital, then located at 131st Street and 10th Avenue.

**JUAN PABLO DUARTE BOULEVARD** The stretch of St. Nicholas Avenue from 162nd to 193rd Streets was named in 2000 to honor a hero of the huge Dominican population in this neighborhood. In 1844 Duarte was one of the leaders of a revolt against domination by Haiti, his country's neighbor on the Caribbean island of Hispaniola.

**JUMEL PLACE & TERRACE** These streets traverse property once owned by French-born wine merchant Stephen Jumel, 1754–1832. The name is better known, however, for its connection with Jumel's beautiful and wily wife, Eliza Brown Bowen Jumel, for whom Jumel bought the 1765 Roger Morris mansion, situated here. A former prostitute, Madame Jumel dumped her husband and in 1833 had a brief and stormy marriage to Aaron Burr, vice president under Thomas Jefferson.

**LAUREL HILL TERRACE** The adjacent hilly landscape was called Laurel Hill at the time of the Revolution, and took its name from the local vegetation.

**MARGARET CORBIN DRIVE & PLAZA** Plucky and brave Margaret Corbin followed her Revolutionary War soldier husband from Pennsylvania to Fort Washington. At the pivotal battle that took place at the fort in 1776, her husband was killed and, nothing daunted, Margaret took his place, (wo)manning a cannon until wounded. She became the first female pensioner of the United States and was granted a yearly suit of clothes and the cash equivalent of a half-pint of liquor monthly for her trouble. Fittingly, she was buried at West Point with full military honors. The thoroughfares were named for her in 1977.

**MCKENNA SQUARE** A mid-street plaza facing the Church of the Rose of Lima on the south and the 33rd Police Precinct on the north honors William J. McKenna of West 173rd Street who died of wounds suffered in World War I.

**MCNALLY PLAZA** Fatalities of World War I are amply represented in this district. Corporal Richard J. McNally of Fort Washington Avenue was killed in action in 1918.

**MITCHEL SQUARE & PARK** When he was elected mayor of the city in 1913, John Purroy Mitchel, 1879–1918, was the youngest person ever to hold that office. He served until 1917, and then joined the Air Corps during which time he was killed falling out of his plane during training in Louisiana.

**NAGLE AVENUE** Jan Nagle (or Nagel) was a 17th-century immigrant from Westphalia. Along with Jan Dyckman (see Dyckman Street above), Nagel bought land here in 1677. Dyckman later married Nagel's widow, thus binding their families and properties together.

**OVERLOOK TERRACE** True to its name, a part of this terrace overlooks the valley to the east.

**PAYSON AVENUE** The Payson in question was Dr. George S. Payson, pastor of the Fort Washington Presbyterian Church from 1880 to 1920.

**PINEHURST AVENUE & SOUTH PINEHURST AVENUE** Landowner C. P. Bucking dubbed his residence here "Pinehurst" and the name survived the bulldozers that leveled the residence.

**PIOTR PINKHASOV PLAZA** The street name bears testimony to the 1970s efforts of the Washington Heights-Inwood Council for Soviet Jewry, chaired by Rabbi Shlomo Kahn, to help Soviet Jews emigrate to Israel and to survive the Soviet system while awaiting visas. Pinkhasov was active in the cause in the USSR and was sent to the Gulag while waiting to leave. He came to the attention of the Council which prevailed on the city to install the sign at 184th Street and Bennett Avenue. It was not long after this public display of support that Pinkhasov was freed and joined his family in Israel.

**PLAZA LAFAYETTE** In the late 19th century the road that ran along the river above 159th Street was called Boulevard LaFayette in honor of the Marquis de LaFayette, French hero of the American Revolution. This traffic plaza retains a remnant of that name.

**POLICE OFFICER FRANCIS X. WALSH STREET** This young officer of the 34th Precinct was killed in 1961 at age 29, having surprised a gunman during a robbery at a grocery store.

**RIVERSIDE DRIVE** Opened as far as 125th Street in 1880, this road winds sinuously along the hilly terrain above the Hudson River, splitting occasionally to embrace the upper "islands" of Riverside Park. The drive was extended at various times until 1925 when it was completed as far as Dyckman Street.

*Marquis de Lafayette*

**ROGER MORRIS PARK** The park in which the Morris-Jumel mansion sits recalls the property's original owner. In 1765 Colonel Morris built the house as a summer retreat on his estate which stretched from river to river. A Loyalist, Morris fled to England early in the Revolution, leaving the house to serve as Washington's headquarters for a month in 1776.

**ST. NICHOLAS AVENUE** The Dutch settlers in New Amsterdam celebrated St. Nicholas Day in December as they had done in their homeland. Washington Irving, author of the fictional *Knickerbocker's History of New York*, is credited with re-popularizing the tradition in 19th-century New York by pronouncing St. Nicholas the patron saint of the city. The avenue was laid out in 1866 on the path of the Albany Post Road.

**SHERMAN AVENUE** The Sherman family were early inhabitants of this locale, residing in what one source describes as a fisherman's dwelling erected circa 1815 at the foot of Fort George Hill. The creek which took the family name emptied into the Harlem River approximately between Dyckman and Academy Streets, and was a well-known local landmark.

**SICKLES STREET** Daniel E. Sickles, 1819 (or 1823 depending on the source) –1914, attended New York University and became a lawyer in the city. He was sheriff of New York County and served in Congress. While in Washington, he discovered that his wife was having an affair with the son of Francis Scott Key, author of the *Star-Spangled Banner*, and he shot him dead. On trial for murder, Sickles was acquitted on grounds of temporary insanity— the first time that defense was used in this country. Sickles entered the Civil War as a brigadier general and saw action in many battles, losing a leg at Gettysburg. From 1869 to 1873 he was minister to Spain where he was known as the "Yankee King of Spain" partly because of his affair with the deposed Queen Isabella of Spain. The last position held by this colorful character was chairman of the New York Monuments Commission, a post from which he was removed on charges of embezzlement.

**STAFF STREET** World War I Sergeant Harry Staff of Sherman Avenue was killed in action in 1918.

**SYLVAN TERRACE** Originally the driveway to the Morris-Jumel mansion (see Jumel Place & Terrace and Roger Morris Park above), this block-long cul-de-sac perched above Amsterdam Avenue is now lined with charming clapboard row houses built in the 1880s. The name no doubt refers to the wooded park to which it leads.

**THAYER STREET** Named in 1911 for Francis Thayer, an attorney, whose dedication to bettering his neighborhood earned him this street name. The Thayer home had previously belonged to the Chittenden family (see Chittenden Avenue above).

**WADSWORTH AVENUE & TERRACE** Born in 1807 in Geneseo, New York, James Samuel Wadsworth was educated at Harvard and Yale, and, though he studied law, he never practiced, preferring to manage his family's 15,000-acre estate in western New York State. Wadsworth was an early member of the Free-Soil party, and an anti-slavery advocate. During the Civil War, though without military training, he served with distinction as a brigadier general and saw action at the first battle of Bull Run, the battles of Fredericksburg and Gettysburg, and was killed during the battle of the Wilderness in 1864. In addition to this avenue, Fort Wadsworth, now the Fort Wadsworth Military Reservation on Staten Island, bears his name.

**WASHINGTON TERRACE** A down-at-the-heels cousin of Sylvan Terrace above, this midblock cul-de-sac near Yeshiva University probably borrowed its name from its neighborhood.

# Inwood
Of all the sections of Manhattan, Inwood is the most redolent of the island primeval. Indian artifacts and cave dwellings were still found here into the 20th century, strong indicators of the importance of this northern extremity in the travels of Native Americans to and from Manhattan Island. The region would become equally important to the Dutch settlers who followed and ultimately drove their native predecessors from their ancestral lands. In the 19th century, the western segment of Inwood was an estate area, and one that did not escape the notice of Central Park designer Frederick Law Olmsted, who urged the powers that were to preserve the area's hilly residential charm. At about the same time, what one source calls "the public taste" selected the name Inwood, an understandable choice given that the former name was Tubby Hook. Though relatively late here, urban development took one form in the eastern, flat section and another in

the western hilly one, creating a bifurcated quality. The subway reached the eastern flank first and tenements were built for Jewish and Irish immigrants. Today, the streets east of Broadway are commercial in nature with elevated subway tracks, car washes, body shops, a depot of the Sanitation Department, and the yards of the New York City Transit Authority. The western blocks have retained a more suburban character, with middle-class apartment buildings and some single-family detached houses tucked away on small side streets. More than a third of this relatively small area is occupied by the lush Inwood Hill and Isham Parks. Olmsted would be thrilled.

ACADEMY STREET  Before Intermediate School 52 was built, an academy located here gave its name to the street.

BEAK STREET  The street was named in 1925 but the Board of Aldermen proceedings give no attribution.

BROADWAY  Originally an Indian trail that ran north from the southern tip of Manhattan, Broadway now extends from the Battery into the Bronx. The street's name derives from its unusual width.

*James Fenimore Cooper*

**COOPER STREET** Named for James Fenimore Cooper, 1789–1851, best known as the author of *The Leatherstocking Tales*, a five-novel series which includes *The Deerslayer* and *The Last of the Mohicans*. Cooper's depictions romanticized American Indians and nature.

**CUMMING STREET** As with Beak Street above, this one was named in 1925 but again the Board of Aldermen proceedings give no attribution.

**DYCKMAN STREET** Jan Dyckman was one of the original property owners in Harlem and bought land near the northern tip of the island in 1677. The Dyckman family holdings in the area grew to be extensive.

**INDIAN ROAD** Artifacts giving evidence of habitation by the Rechgawawanc Indians abounded here into the first quarter of the 20th century. It is thought that this road follows the path of an Indian trail leading from Spuyten Duyvil—the strait which connected the Harlem and the Hudson Rivers—to an Indian village.

**INWOOD HILL PARK** The fact that the real estate on the hill was owned by a few private individuals until it was converted to a park accounts for the preservation of the area's lushly wooded topography. The city acquired the land in stages from 1915 to 1941 after years of pressure on the part of citizens and politicians adamant that the wild landscape not be developed. The park was opened for the first time in 1917.

**ISHAM STREET & PARK** The street was named for William B. Isham who acquired his estate here in 1864. The land for the park was given to the city by Isham's daughter.

**LIEUTENANT WILLIAM TIGHE TRIANGLE** A traffic garden pays tribute to a World War II soldier.

**MONSIGNOR FRANCIS J. KETT PLAZA** Named in 1970, the plaza honors the founder and first pastor of St. Jude's Roman Catholic Church.

**NAGLE AVENUE** Jan Nagle (or Nagel) was a 17th-century immigrant from Westphalia. Along with Jan Dyckman (see Dyckman Street above), Nagel bought land here in 1677. Dyckman later married Nagel's widow, thus binding their families and properties together.

**PARK TERRACE EAST & WEST** These streets traverse the hill overlooking Isham Park.

**PAYSON AVENUE** The Payson in question was Dr. George S. Payson, pastor of the Fort Washington Presbyterian Church from 1880 to 1920.

**POST AVENUE** The Post family acquired land here in 1810, and their progeny intermarried with other local families, among them the Nagels.

**RIVERSIDE DRIVE** Opened as far as 125th Street in 1880, this road winds sinuously along the hilly terrain above the Hudson River, splitting occasionally to embrace the upper "islands" of Riverside Park. The drive was extended at various times until 1925 when it was completed as far as Dyckman Street.

**SEAMAN AVENUE** John and Valentine Seaman, whose father, Valentine Sr., was a prominent 18th-century physician, owned property here. Valentine's house was on the hill overlooking Isham Park.

**SHERMAN AVENUE** The Sherman family were early residents of this locale, residing in what one source describes as a fisherman's dwelling erected circa 1815 at the foot of Fort George Hill. The creek which took the family name emptied into the Harlem River approximately between Dyckman and Academy Streets, and was a well-known local landmark.

**VERMILYEA AVENUE** Isaac Vermeille was a Huguenot refugee from Leyden who brought his family to New Amsterdam in 1663. They settled in New Harlem, succeeded and proliferated, and became an important local family with a slightly altered surname.

# Marble Hill

Once upon a time, the north-eastern section of Inwood protruded north from Manhattan Island in a shape not unlike that of a piano. This northernmost reach of the island was a rocky promontory called Marble Hill, a name conferred in the late 19th century which referred to the marble (actually limestone) quarries around its base. Spuyten Duyvil Creek wound lazily around Marble Hill's northern protuberance, connecting the Harlem and the Hudson Rivers. As early as 1826 the legislature chartered a canal company to cut a channel from Spuyten Duyvil to the Harlem River, deepening, straightening, and eradicating the sinuous and shallow Spuyten Duyvil Creek. The first section of the canal was opened in 1895, allowing ships access from the Hudson River to Long Island Sound and eliminating the longer trip around the Battery. This engineering feat amputated Marble Hill from the body of Manhattan, and grafted it onto the Bronx. In a scenario that could probably only happen in New York, Marble Hill remains politically part of the borough of Manhattan, though physically located in the Bronx. The street names date way back, and reflect the layering of land ownership, with successive generations and families imprinting their names here. As with other northern sections of the city, Marble Hill remained a bit of a backwater until the subway made the trip here from lower Manhattan manageable. Today the hill is a quirky and compact hodgepodge of detached houses and apartment buildings clinging to its vertiginous slopes, the southern part of which enjoys a captivating view of the river and the opposite shore of Manhattan. Not surprisingly, the neighborhood retains a curious never-never-land quality of having alighted here from some other time and place.

**ADRIAN AVENUE**  It is said that this street harks back to Adriaen Van der Donck, 17th-century Dutch immigrant and lawyer who was granted permission to buy land here from the Indians in 1646.

**BROADWAY**  Originally an Indian trail that ran north from the southern tip of Manhattan, Broadway now extends from the Battery into the Bronx. The street's name derives from its unusual width.

**FORT CHARLES PLACE**  In 1776 the American rebels erected a fort here to control the King's Bridge which was situated nearby and connected the Bronx and Manhattan. The fort was taken by Hessian soldiers and named by them in honor of Charles, Prince of Brunswick, brother-in-law of England's King George.

**HENRY RIVERA PLACE**  Described by local residents as a neighborhood hero, Henry Rivera was killed in 1995 attempting to intervene in a holdup of a local laundromat.

**JACOBUS PLACE**  A name reminiscent of northern Manhattan's early Dutch days, this street honors the great-grandson of Jan Dyckman (see Washington Heights and Inwood). Jacobus Dyckman III inherited extensive property and bought what became known as Marble Hill. He and his family were esteemed and influential residents of these areas.

**KINGSBRIDGE AVENUE**  The original path was that of an Indian trail leading from the southern tip of Manhattan to the Bronx and thence north. With European settlers making greater use of the route, it was gradually improved and became known as the King's Road. In 1693 the first bridge to cross the water separating Manhattan and the Bronx was constructed. It was called the King's Bridge—in honor of King William III—and prompted the road to be called the King's Bridge Road, and the settlement nearby—now Marble Hill—to be named Kingsbridge. The bridge was subsequently covered over by what is now Kingsbridge Avenue.

**MARBLE HILL AVENUE & LANE**  Named for the neighborhood they traverse.

**TERRACE VIEW AVENUE**  Geographically descriptive, the avenue follows a terrace of Marble Hill.

**TEUNISSEN PLACE**  Tobias Teunissen, a wool washer and a 1636 immigrant from Leyden in Holland, was the first white settler—actually a squatter—in this locale. He and all but his wife and one child were killed during an Indian raid in 1655. It was his land that the "Jans"— Nagel and Dyckman (see Washington Heights and Inwood)—bought in 1677.

**TIBBETT AVENUE**  Originally Tippett, for George Tippett, a 17th-century settler in the neighborhood who left his surname on a brook and a hill. The spelling has suffered in the course of centuries.

**VAN CORLEAR PLACE** Anthony Van Corlear—also spelled Van Curler—was an early area resident.

# Perimeter Routes It is hard,

now, to imagine Manhattan without its perimeter of highways.

Three of these routes were conceived and hauled into exis-

tence through the vision and perseverance of Robert Moses as

head of the Triborough Bridge and Tunnel Authority. In addi-

tion to cleaning up the ragged waterfronts, described in many

of the introductory paragraphs above, these arteries have made

it possible, sometimes, to circle the island with speed and effi-

ciency. They have also, for the most part, contributed to the

age-old Manhattan tradition of turning the city's focus inward

toward the center as opposed to outward toward the water.

Despite the conviction expressed in the Commissioners' Plan

of 1811 that Manhattan, blessed with nature's watery girdle,

required a minimum of planned parks and open spaces, until

recently we have taken little advantage of this gift. Too often

green spaces and esplanades are squeezed between the roadway and the water, and access to them is difficult or danger-

ous. Though scant room remains to reverse this course, efforts

such as the esplanade at Battery Park City, Hudson River Park,

and the cleaning of the rivers will hopefully turn Manhattan's

eyes and feet outward and across its perimeter routes.

FRANKLIN DELANO ROOSEVELT / EAST RIVER DRIVE  Commonly known simply as
"The FDR," this artery stretches from lower Manhattan up the shore of the East River to the
Harlem River Drive. Work began in 1938, not long after completion of the Triborough
Bridge, and was finished in 1942. The route was named for the president and the river that
it skirts.

HARLEM RIVER DRIVE  The oldest part of the drive was opened in 1898 and ran from
155th Street and St. Nicholas Place to the Harlem River, and then north along the river to
Dyckman Street. This section was called the Harlem Speedway or Driveway, and was part of
a larger "pleasure drive" conceived in 1902 which looped down as far as Central Park West
and 72nd Street. The Speedway, which took its name from the adjacent Harlem River, was
extended to connect with the new FDR Drive in the 1930s.

HENRY HUDSON PARKWAY  The parkway, opened in 1936, runs from West 72nd Street
along the Hudson River and across the Henry Hudson Bridge to Westchester County. It was
constructed as part of Robert Moses's West Side Improvement Project, and, like the river, is
named for the explorer who sailed up the river in 1609.

JOE DIMAGGIO HIGHWAY  Previously called the West Side Highway, the route extending from the Battery along the Hudson River to West 72nd Street was renamed in 1999 to
honor the great New York Yankee baseball player who had recently died.

# Illustration Sources

ALL BACKGROUND MAPS *(pp. 6,*
*22, 48, 75, 93, 111, 126, 139, 166)*
*Map of the five Cities of New York, Brooklyn,*
*Jersey City, Hoboken and Hudson City.*
*(details)*
Scale [ca. 1:24,000]
[New York?] : M. Dripps, 1860
Bancroft G3804.N4 1860.D7 Case XD
no.1 and no.2
Courtesy of the Bancroft Library
University of California, Berkeley

INTRODUCTION PAGE *(p. 10–11)*
*New York City Skyline taken south of Statue*
*of Liberty*
Photo: The Port of New York Authority,
10/7/53
Museum of the City of New York
Print Archives

ADOLPH S. OCHS STREET
*(p. 118)*
*Adolph S. Ochs*
Photograph by Pirie MacDonald
*The Dictionary of American Portraits*
Dover Publications Inc., New York,
1967

ALLEN STREET *(p. 50)*
*The Pelican Sloop of War, Capt. Maples,*
*Raking & Capturing the American Brig.*
*Argus*
W. B. Walker, mezzotint, 1813
Negative #49967
Collection of the New-York Historical
Society

ASTOR PLACE *(p. 64)*
*John Jacob Astor*
Swan Electric Engraving Co. after
Gilbert Stuart painting, photogravure,
1899
Negative #57707
Collection of the New-York Historical
Society

AUDUBON AVENUE *(p. 169)*
*John Audubon*
Portrait
Museum of the City of New York
Print Archives

AVENUE OF THE FINEST *(p. 34)*
*John Grafton*
*New York in the 19th Century*
Dover Publications Inc., New York,
1980

BARUCH DRIVE & PLACE *(p. 51)*
*Simon Baruch*
Courtesy of New York University
Medical Center
*The Dictionary of American Portraits*
Dover Publications Inc., New York, 1967

BATTERY PLACE & PARK *(p. 25)*
*Battery Place*
Reproduction, n.d.
Museum of the City of New York
Print Archives

BEEKMAN PLACE *(p. 113)*
*The Beekman House, Headquarters of Sir*
*William Howe*
Sarony, Major and Knapp, lithograph,
1861
Negative #54215
Collection of the New-York Historical
Society

BRIDGE STREET *(p. 25)*
*Broad Street Bridge, 1659*
unidentified artist, 1898
Negative #1255
Collection of the New-York Historical
Society

BRYANT PARK *(p. 105)*
*William Cullen Bryant*
Henry Peters Gray, oil on canvas,
ca. 1815
Negative #6375
Collection of the New-York Historical
Society

ERICSSON PLACE *(p. 44)*
John Ericsson
Samuel Hollyer, engraving
The Dictionary of American Portraits
Dover Publications Inc., New York, 1967

FORT WASHINGTON AVENUE & PARK
*(p. 171)*
George Washington
John Grafton
The American Revolution
Dover Publications Inc., New York, 1975

FREDERICK DOUGLASS CIRCLE
*(p. 163)*
Frederick Douglass
Photograph #SC-CN-80-0455
Photographs and Prints Division
Schomburg Center for Research in
BlackCulture
The New York Public Library
Astor, Lenox and Tilden Foundations

FULTON STREET *(p. 27)*
Steamboat Clermont *or* North River
Richard Varick DeWitt, watercolor, 1861
Negative #38716
Collection of the New-York Historical
Society

GANDHI GARDEN *(p. 97)*
Mahatma Gandhi
National Gandhi Museum
New Delhi, India

GENERAL DOUGLAS MACARTHUR
PLAZA & MACARTHUR PARK
*(p. 114)*
Douglas MacArthur (detail)
Courtesy of the FDR Library
Hyde Park, New York

GREELEY SQUARE *(p. 105)*
Horace Greeley
The Dictionary of American Portraits
Dover Publications Inc., New York, 1967

HAMILTON FISH PARK *(p. 53)*
Hamilton Fish
Picture Collection
The Branch Libraries
The New York Public Library

HAMILTON TERRACE & PLACE
*(p. 163)*
Alexander Hamilton
J. F. E. Prud'homme, engraving from a
painting by Archibald Robertson
The Dictionary of American Portraits
Dover Publications Inc., New York, 1967

HOWARD STREET *(p. 69)*
The American Fireman: Rushing to the Conflict
Louis Maurer, colored lithograph, 1858
Museum of the City of New York
Harry T. Peters Collection, 56.300.6

JACK DEMPSEY CORNER *(p. 119)*
Jack Dempsey
Photograph, n.d.
Museum of the City of New York
Print Archives/Sports-Boxing

JACKIE ROBINSON PARK *(p. 155)*
Jackie Robinson
Photograph #SC-CN-80-0308
Photographs and Prints Division
Schomburg Center for Research in Black
Culture
The New York Public Library
Astor, Lenox and Tilden Foundations

JAMES J. WALKER PARK *(p. 91)*
James J. Walker
Photograph by Pach Bros., ca. 1925
Negative #49518
Collection of the New-York Historical
Society

JAY STREET *(p. 45)*
John Jay
John Grafton
The American Revolution
Dover Publications Inc., New York, 1975

JEFFERSON STREET *(p. 53)*
Thomas Jefferson
John Grafton
The American Revolution
Dover Publications Inc., New York, 1975

JOE LOUIS PLAZA *(p. 110)*
*Joseph Barrow Louis*
Enit Kaufman, crayon on paper, ca.1940
Negative #30619
Collection of the New-York Historical
Society

JOHN JAY PARK *(p. 131)*
*John Jay*
John Grafton
*The American Revolution*
Dover Publications Inc., New York, 1975

JUMEL PLACE & TERRACE *(p. 172)*
*Jumel Mansion, West 160th Street*
Lithograph
Museum of the City of New York
Print Archives

LA GUARDIA PLACE *(p. 82)*
*Fiorello La Guardia, n.d.*
Unident. photographer from Daily News
Negative # 73998
Collection of the New-York Historical
Society

LANGSTON HUGHES PLACE *(p. 135)*
*Langston Hughes*
Photograph #SC-CN-80-0344
Photographs and Prints Division
Schomburg Center for Research in Black
Culture
The New York Public Library
Astor, Lenox and Tilden Foundations

LENOX AVENUE *(p. 156)*
*James Lenox*
Portrait
Museum of the City of New York
Print Archives

MACDOUGAL STREET *(p. 70)*
*Major General Alexander MacDougall*
John Ramage, miniature on ivory, n.d.
Negative #37340
Collection of the New-York Historical
Society

MADISON SQUARE PARK *(p. 106)*
*Hand of the Statue of Liberty*
H.E., engraving, 1877
Negative #58112
Collection of the New-York Historical
Society

MADISON STREET *(p. 39)*
*James Madison*
Picture Collection
The Branch Libraries
The New York Public Library

MARCUS GARVEY PARK *(p. 136)*
*Marcus Garvey*
Photograph #SC-CN-80-0040
Photographs and Prints Division
Schomburg Center for Research in Black
Culture
The New York Public Library
Astor, Lenox and Tilden Foundations

MARY MCLEOD BETHUNE PLACE
*(p. 157)*
*Mary McLeod Bethune*
Photograph #SC-CN-80-0309
Photographs and Prints Division
Schomburg Center for Research in Black
Culture
The New York Public Library
Astor, Lenox and Tilden Foundations

MULBERRY STREET *(p. 66)*
*Morus nigra, black mulberry*
J. G. Heck
*The Complete Encyclopedia of Illustration*
Random House Value Publishing, Inc., 1996

NELSON & WINNIE MANDELA
CORNER *(p. 101)*
*Nelson Mandela (detail)*
Courtesy of the U.N. Photo Library
UN/DPI Photo by Greg Kinch, copyright
United Nations

OLD SLIP *(p. 28)*
*South Street at Old Slip on East River Waterfront*
Unidentified photographer, ca.1905
Negative #49128
Collection of the New-York Historical
Society

**PEARL STREET** *(p. 29)*
*Ostrea cristigalli*
J. G. Heck
*The Complete Encyclopedia of Illustration*
Random House Value Publishing, Inc., 1996

**PIERRE TOUSSAINT SQUARE** *(p. 29)*
*Pierre Toussaint*
Anthony Meucci, miniature on ivory, ca.1825
Negative #2841
Collection of the New-York Historical
Society

**PIKE STREET & SLIP** *(p. 62)*
*Zebulon M. Pike (detail)*
J. Kennedy, engraving, ca. 1813
Negative #45320
Collection of the New-York Historical
Society

**PLAZA LAFAYETTE** *(p. 174)*
*Marquis de Lafayette*
John Grafton
*The American Revolution*
Dover Publications Inc., New York, 1975

**POMANDER WALK** *(p. 148)*
Photograph by Michael Feirstein

**RAOUL WALLENBERG WALK** *(p. 115)*
*Raoul Wallenberg*
Courtesy of the Raoul Wallenberg
Committee of the United States

**RIVINGTON STREET** *(p. 54)*
*Rivington's New-York Gazetteer, Declaration of*
*Loyalty to George III*
Rivington, newspaper, April 20, 1775
Negative #52893
Collection of the New-York Historical
Society

**RUNYON'S WAY** *(p. 125)*
*Damon Runyon (detail)*
Photograph from B File:Runyon, Damon
Billy Rose Theatre Collection
The New York Public Library for the
Performing Arts
Astor, Lenox and Tilden Foundations

**ST. JOHN'S LANE** *(p. 46)*
*St. John's Chapel, View from the Park (detail)*
W. D. Smith after A. J. Davis, engraving, 1829
Negative #4235
Collection of the New-York Historical
Society

**ST. MARK'S PLACE** *(p. 79)*
*St. Mark's Church, Second Ave. & 10th Street*
Unidentified artist, 1898
Negative #32870
Collection of the New-York Historical
Society

**ST. NICHOLAS AVENUE** *(p. 158)*
*Washington Irving*
Portrait
Museum of the City of New York
Print Archives

**SARA DELANO ROOSEVELT PARK**
*(p. 62)*
*Sara Delano Roosevelt*
Courtesy of the FDR Library
Hyde Park, New York

**SEWARD PARK** *(p. 55)*
*William Henry Seward*
Picture Collection
The Branch Libraries
The New York Public Library

**STUYVESANT SQUARE** *(p. 98)*
*Peter Stuyvesant*
Charles Burt, engraving
*The Dictionary of American Portraits*
Dover Publications Inc., New York, 1967

**THEODORE ROOSEVELT PARK** *(p. 149)*
*Theodore Roosevelt*
*The Dictionary of American Portraits*
Dover Publications Inc., New York, 1967

**THOMAS PAINE PARK** *(p. 40)*
*Title Page of* Common Sense, *by Thomas Paine*
W. & T. Bradford, printers, pamphlet, 1776
Negative #23729
Collection of the New-York Historical
Society

TRINITY PLACE *(p. 30)*
*Trinity Church*
Drawing, 1859
Museum of the City of New York
Print Archives

YITZHAK RABIN WAY *(p. 102)*
*Yitzhak Rabin (detail)*
Courtesy of the U.N. Photo Library
UN/DPI photo by Evan Schneider, copyright
United Nations

UNION SQUARE *(p. 98)*
*Union Square*
J. Bornet, lithograph, 1850
Museum of the City of New York
J. Clarence Davies Collection, 29.100.1950

UNIVERSITY PLACE *(p. 87)*
*New York University and Washington Square*
Henry Hoff, lithograph, ca. 1850
Negative #8201
Collection of the New-York Historical
Society

VANDERBILT AVENUE *(p. 121)*
*Cornelius Vanderbilt*
Alexander H. Ritchie, engraving
*The Dictionary of American Portraits*
Dover Publications Inc., New York, 1967

WALL STREET *(p. 31)*
Picture Collection
The Branch Libraries
The New York Public Library

WASHINGTON MARKET PARK *(p. 47)*
*Vignettes at the Old Washington Market (detail)*
Unidentified artist, engraving, August 3, 1883
Negative #67098
Collection of the New-York Historical
Society

WAVERLY PLACE *(p. 92)*
*Sir Walter Scott*
Picture Collection
The Branch Libraries
The New York Public Library

WORTH STREET *(p. 41)*
*William Jenkins Worth*
John Sartain, engraving
*The Dictionary of American Portraits*
Dover Publications Inc., New York, 1967

Illustration Sources

# Works Consulted

The Alleys of New York. Forgotten New York Website (http://www.forgotten-ny.com).

Atlas of the City of New York, Borough of Manhattan. New York: G.W. Bromley, various years.

Bancker, Evert Jr. Bancker's Surveying Records 1780–1795; 1798–1815. Manuscript Collection of the New-York Historical Society.

Baron, Stanley Wade. Brewed in America. Boston: Little, Brown, 1962.

Barr, Lockwood. The Hunter Desbrosses and Allied Families of New York City and Hunter's Island. typescript, 1945. New York Public Library, Local History and Genealogy Division.

Barr, Phyllis. "History of Street Names." Trinity Life, July 1985.

Belle, John, and Maxine R. Leighton. Grand Central. New York: Norton, 2000.

Bolton, Reginald Pelham. Washington Heights. New York: Dyckman Institute, 1924.

Bridenbaugh, Carl. Cities in the Wilderness. New York: The Ronald Press, 1938.

Brown, Henry Collins, ed. Valentine's Manual of Old New York. New York: The Chauncey Holt Co., 1925.

Bulloch, Joseph G. B. A History and Genealogy of the Families of Bayard, Houstoun of Georgia. Washington, D. C.: J. H. Dony, 1919.

Burrows, Edwin G., and Mike Wallace. Gotham, A History of New York City to 1898. New York: Oxford University Press, 1999.

Buttenwieser, Ann. Manhattan Water Bound. New York: New York University Press, 1987.

Cannistraro, Philip V., ed. The Italians of New York. New York: The New York Historical Society, 1999.

Carlisle, Robert J., ed. Records and Biographical Sketches. New York: Society of Alumni of Bellevue Hospital, Press of Charles Edgar, 1929.

Carnog, Evan. The Birth of Empire, De Witt Clinton and the American Experience 1769–1828. New York: Oxford University Press, 1998.

Caro, Robert. The Power Broker. New York: Random House, 1975.

Cohen, Paul E., and Robert T. Augustyn. Manhattan in Maps. New York: Rizzoli, 1997.

"Columbus and Amsterdam Avenues." Real Estate Record and Builders' Guide, Vol. 45, March 22, 1890, p. 399.

Cook, Leland A. St. Patrick's Cathedral. New York: Quick Fox, 1979.

Cooke, Hope. Seeing New York: History Walks for Armchair and Footloose Travelers. Philadelphia: Temple University Press, 1995.

Countryman, Edward. A People in Revolution. Baltimore: Johns Hopkins University Press, 1981.

Dajani, Virginia. *Juror's Guide to Lower Manhattan.* New York: Municipal Art Society, 1990.

Dolkart, Andrew S. *Guide to New York City Landmarks.* Washington, D. C.: The Preservation Press, National Trust for Historic Preservation, 1992.

Dolkart, Andrew S. *Morningside Heights.* New York: Columbia University Press, 1998.

Dolkart, Andrew, S., and Gretchen S. Sorin. *Touring Historic Harlem, Four Walks in Northern Manhattan.* New York: New York Landmarks Conservancy, 1997.

Dolkart, Andrew S. *Touring the Upper East Side, Walks in Five Historic Districts.* New York: New York Landmarks Conservancy, 1995.

Downs, Winfield Scott, ed. *Who's Who in New York.* New York: Who's Who Publications, 1929.

Dunshee, Kenneth Holcomb. *As You Pass By.* New York: Hastings House Publishers, 1952.

*Early Columbia Engineers: An Appreciation.* New York: Columbia University Press, 1929.

Falk, Byron A. Jr., and Valerie R. Falk, eds. *Personal Name Index to New York Times Index, 1851–1974.* Verdi, Nevada: Roxbury Data Interface, 1982.

Falk, Byron A., Jr., and Valerie R. Falk, eds. *Personal Name Index to New York Times Index, 1975–1989.* Verdi, Nevada: Roxbury Data Interface, 1991.

Faragher, John Mack, ed. *The Encyclopedia of Colonial and Revolutionary America.* New York: Facts on File, 1990.

Flexner, James Thomas. *George Washington in the American Revolution (1775–1783).* Boston: Little, Brown, 1968.

Garraty, John A., and Mark C. Carnes, eds. *American National Biography.* New York: Oxford University Press, 1999.

Gayle, Margot, and Michele Cohen. *The Art Commission and the Municipal Art Society Guide to Manhattan's Outdoor Sculpture.* New York: Prentice Hall Press, 1988.

Gold, Joyce, *From Trout Stream to Bohemia,* New York: Old Warren Road Press, 1988.

Goodwin, Doris Kearns. *No Ordinary Time, Franklin & Eleanor Roosevelt: The Home Front in World War II.* New York: Simon & Schuster, 1995.

Gray, Christopher. *Changing New York, the Architectural Scene.* New York: Dover Publications, 1992.

Gray, Christopher. "History of the Upper East Side." *Avenue Magazine,* September 1985.

Gray, Christopher. *Sutton Place, Uncommon Community by the River.* New York: Sutton Area Community, 1997.

*Greenwich Village Guide.* New York: The Villager, 1939.

Hamm, Margherita A. *Famous Families of New York.* New York: Heraldic Publishing, 1970.

Harrington, Virginia D. *The New York Merchant on the Eve of the Revolution.* New York: Columbia University Press, 1935.

*Historical Signs.* City of New York / Parks & Recreation Website (http://www.nyc.gov/parks).

Holgate, Jerome B. *American Genealogy, Being a History of Some of the Early Settlers of North America.* Albany, New York: J. Munsell, 1848.

Homberger, Eric. *The Historical Atlas of New York City.* New York: Henry Holt, 1994.

Honan, William H., ed. *Greenwich Village Guide.* New York: The Bryan Publications, 1959.

Humphrey, David C. *From King's College to Columbia 1746–1800.* New York: Columbia University Press, 1976.

*Insurance Maps of the City of New York.* New York: Perris and Browne, various years.

Jackson, Kenneth T., ed. *The Encyclopedia of New York City.* New Haven, Connecticut: Yale University Press, 1995.

Kaminski, John P. *George Clinton, Yeoman Politician of the New Republic.* Madison, Wisconsin: Madison House Publishers, 1993.

Kelley, Frank Bergen, comp. *Historical Guide to the City of New York from the Original Observations and Contributions Made by Members and Friends of the City History Club of New York.* New York: Frederick Stokes, 1909.

Knox, Herman W., ed. *Who's Who in New York.* New York: Who's Who Publications, 1918.

"Lispenard-Witherbee and Allied Families." *Americana Illustrated,* Vol. 14. New York: The American Historical Society, 1920, pp. 262-273.

Lockwood, Charles. *Bricks and Brownstone.* New York: Abbeville Press, 1972.

Lockwood, Charles. *Manhattan Moves Uptown.* New York: Barnes & Noble, 1976.

Ludwig, John W. *Alphabet of Greatness,* typescript 1961. New York Public Library, Local History and Genealogy Division.

*Manhattan City Directories,* various years.

Martin, Lawrence. *History of the General Society of Mechanics and Tradesmen of the City of New York.* New York: The General Society of Mechanics and Tradesmen, n.d.

Melvers, Helen Howard. *Genealogy of the Renwick Family.* n.p., 1924.

Mendelsohn, Joyce. *Touring the Flatiron, Walks in Four Historic Neighborhoods.* New York: New York Landmarks Conservancy, 1998.

Mendelsohn, Joyce. "Why Houston Street?" *The New York Chronicle,* Vol. 10, No. 1, Fall/Winter 1997.

*Minutes of the Common Council 1784–1831.* New York: The City of New York, 1917.

*The New York Times Obituaries Index, 1858–1968.* New York: The New York Times, 1970.

*The New York Times Obituaries Index, 1969–1978.* New York: The New York Times, 1980.

*Proceedings of the City Council of the City of New York,* Published by Authority of the Council, various years.

The Real Estate Record Association. *History of Real Estate, Building and Architecture in New York City During the Last Quarter of a Century.* 1898. Reprint, New York: Arno Press, 1967.

Reps, John W. *The Making of Urban America.* Princeton, New Jersey: Princeton University Press, 1992.

"A Review of West Side Progress." *Real Estate Record and Builders' Guide,* Vol 46, Supplement, December 20, 1890.

*Sanborn Manhattan Land Book of the City of New York.* Weehawken, New Jersey: First American Real Estate Solutions, 1999–2000.

Sandberg, Carl. *Abraham Lincoln.* New York: Charles Scribner's Sons, 1949.

Schomburg Center for Research in Black Culture. *The Black New Yorkers.* New York: John Wiley, 2000.

Shannon, Joseph. *Manual of the Corporation of the City of New York.* New York: E. Jones & Co., Printers, 1869.

Shelton, Hal T. *General Richard Montgomery and the American Revolution.* New York: New York University Press, 1994.

Sobel, Robert, and John Raimo. *Biographical Directory of the Governors of the United States 1789–1978.* Westport, Connecticut: Meckler Books, 1978.

Stern, Robert A. M., Gregory Gilmartin, and John Massengale. *New York 1900.* New York: Rizzoli International, 1992.

Stokes, I.N. Phelps. *The Iconography of Manhattan Island.* 1915–1928. Reprint, Union, New Jersey: The Lawbook Exchange, 1998.

"Street Names." *New York Genealogical and Biographical Record,* Vol. 20. New York: Berkeley Lyceum, 1889, p. 65.

Tauranac, John. *Essential New York.* New York: Holt, Rinehart and Winston, 1979.

Tucker, Glenn. *Poltoons and Patriots.* Indianapolis: Bobbs-Merrill, 1954.

Ulmann, Albert. *A Landmark History of New York.* New York: Appleton and Company, 1906.

Valentine, D. T. *Manual of the Corporation of the City of New York.* New York: McSpedon & Baker, Printers, 1852 and 1855.

*Who Was Who in America 1607–1896.* Chicago: Marquis-Who's Who, 1963.

Willensky, Elliot, and Norval White. *AIA Guide to New York City,* New York: Harcourt Brace Jovanovich, 1988.

Williams, C. S. *Andrew Cannon and His Descendants 1651–1912.* New York: C. S. Williams, 1912.

*World Book Encyclopedia.* Chicago: World Book, 1994.

*The WPA Guide to New York City.* 1939. Reprint, New York: The New Press, 1992.

Yoshpe, Harry B. *The Disposition of Loyalist Estates in the Southern District of the State of New York.* New York: AMS Press, 1967.

# Index